LEADERSHIP
TRANSITIONS
FOR GROWTH

LEADERSHIP
TRANSITIONS
FOR GROWTH

MICHAEL FLETCHER

WAGNER
PUBLICATIONS

Leadership Transitions for Growth
Copyright © 2003 by Michael Fletcher
ISBN 1-58502-037-0

Published by
Wagner Publications
11005 N. Highway 83
Colorado Springs, CO 80921
www.wagnerpublications.org

Cover design by
Imagestudios
100 East St. Suite 105
Colorado Springs, CO 80903
719-578-0351 www.imagestudios.net

Edit and interior design by
Rebecca Sytsema

Rights for publishing this book in other languages are contracted by Gospel Literature International (GLINT). For further information, contact GLINT, P.O. Box 4060, Ontario, CA 91761-1003, USA. You may also send e-mail to glintint@aol.com, or visit their web site at www.glint.org.

1 2 3 4 5 6 7 8 9   09 08 07 06 05 04 03

TABLE OF CONTENTS

FOREWORD

Most pastors in America and in other countries where Christian churches exist will spend a career of 30 or 40, or whatever number of years, pastoring small churches. Around 90 percent of them will never see a regular Sunday attendance of over 200, give or take a few. The average weekly church attendance in America is well under 100.

Surfacing facts like these are in no way intended to put down small church pastors. They are essential for the body of Christ to be all that God intends it to be. Heavenly awards for pastors will not be distributed from the top to the bottom of a list of church sizes. Many small church pastors will end up having more stars in their crown than some of the megachurch pastors who have become household names.

God will reward pastors, as He will all believers, on the basis of how, in this life, they exercised faithful stewardship of the gifts that He gave them. Because small churches are essential for the health of the collective body of Christ, God has chosen to gift many pastors as small church pastors. Most small church pastors are right where they are supposed to be.

But not all. Some small church pastors have been given the necessary gifts to lead larger churches, but for different reasons they have not been able to move into their true destiny. Here is where this book comes into the picture. Michael Fletcher, whose church numbers in the thousands, has personally broken the barriers that ordinarily stall out church attendance. Most others like him, who have also broken the barriers, are the kind who lead so intuitively that, if you asked them, they would not have a clue as to how they made it happen. They would say, "It was just the grace of God," or words to that effect—words which offer little or no practical guidance to others who desire to follow in their footsteps.

Michael Fletcher is different. Not only does he have what it takes to pastor a large church, but he also has the ability to analyze how he got there and to spell it out clearly for others. If you are a pastor or church leader, and if you are not satisfied with the status quo, this book will be a tremendous help and encouragement to you.

Let me make a couple of comments about this book.

First, I would point out that the Church Growth Movement is now almost forty years old. Researchers throughout that period have discovered that there are actual numerical barriers to the growth of a local congregation, and different ones have postulated, let's say, about a dozen of these supposed barriers. Only two have withstood the test of time, the 100/200 barrier and the 700/800 barrier. This book is totally up to date. It is the first church growth book to focus on these two proven barriers to church growth.

My second comment may sound like hyperbole, but it is not. Of the hundreds of books that have been published on church growth, I would say that this is the best guidebook for pastors today. For one thing, it brings together the wisdom of years and applies it to twenty-first century churches. It is better than any of my church growth books, because my books are now considered old. For another, Michael Fletcher has a commendable ability to carve away the fat and get right down to the meat. A superb quality of this book is its compact size with power-packed information on each page. As you read it, I promise that you will not feel like you are wasting time.

Have you reached your full destiny as a church leader? *Leadership Transitions for Growth* will help you answer that question and will show you how to move forward to a new level.

C. Peter Wagner
Senior Professor of Church Growth
Fuller Theological Seminary

GOD HAS A PLAN FOR YOU AND YOUR CHURCH

When a new church begins, it is often planted by those who, in the early days, do everything as friends. The church is their mutual project and they "own it" together. The core people arrive early on Sundays to set up the chairs. Because the sound system lives in the worship leader's trunk, that person is always the first to arrive and unlock all the doors in the rented facility. (Except that one time he was on vacation and took the whole system to the beach.) When folks arrive, everyone knows everyone else by name—even the children are known by everyone! It's easy to spot newcomers who are usually swarmed upon and talked about over lunch. Sometimes they may actually become lunch. It is also easy to tell if someone is missing. There simply are no cracks through which anyone can fall. When a mom is sick or gives birth, no meals have to be organized—friends just show up with a dish.

And relationships grow and strengthen as the early challenges are overcome.

Need more space? No problem, the men of the church give up their Saturday afternoon and bust out a wall or two to make more room for the kids or to add more chairs for worshipers. Sunday after church it's potluck ("blessing" in some churches—they don't do "luck"), as all the folks man the paint brushes to coat the newly constructed, but not-quite-so-straight walls. Some paint and some point out missed spots, but while the paint goes on the walls (and some on the floor), painters and pointers alike dream aloud of the days when the church will really grow.

"This is church life as it was meant to be!" Everything is perfect. You can always get to the pastor, you know everyone by name, you make the sacrifices necessary to make the church better. Yes, everything is perfect—until the one thing happens that can ruin it all. New people come, and now they tend to stay. No one can remember when it started to happen. One day you came in and it seemed that the place was full—new faces without names. And children? "Not sure, but I wonder if the parents are serving in the nursery." Everyone is supposed to take their turn, but not everyone does, so before long a leader is appointed to make sure everyone is on some sort of list, and the new people are duly instructed. There are too many chairs for the committed few to set out, so a special team is formed. A list appears in the bulletin (never had bulletins in the early days—too unspiritual) of people who are scheduled to clean the building, since the four ladies who used to do it every week needed a break.

In one area after another, leaders are appointed, and teams are formed to facilitate the flow of ministry. The church is growing but no one knows why. Worse yet, no one knows what will stop that growth. Who has time to ask questions like that? There are meetings to be held and new leaders to be raised up.

Soon elders are put into place to help the pastor carry the load. At first, that is their only assignment—help carry the load. But what does that mean? Does an elder's role ever change? It seems like Scripture indicates that having elders in place will help the church grow. And it isn't long before that starts to prove true. With elders in place, helping "carry the load"—that is doing the ministry—the pastor has more time to be creative, and the people get more of the attention they crave. The church happily grows on. What used to be "owned" by everyone is now "owned" by the elders, and the people concede that to them. After all, they have been the ones who were there from the beginning and made the greatest sacrifices. Great people with great families, they, along with the pastor, have the authority in the church. They can do anything —even stop its growth.

Stop its growth?! Why would they want to do that? The truth is, they don't want to stop its growth, but they will. They are totally unaware that a barrier to growth awaits them—a barrier caused by their own success. They not only create the barrier, but are at the same time, the key to getting over it! If the pastor and elders will adjust the way they relate together in leadership and realign some of the internal structures they built into the church, they can keep right on growing. Most churches don't make those adjustments for two reasons: 1. they don't see the barrier, so they don't see the need, and 2. they don't want to change what they perceive made them successful in the first place.

This is where the trouble starts. The church slows in its growth, even though it continues to slowly add people. Unfortunately, folks leave at about the same pace as others are added. Under the surface, frustration mounts, especially among the leaders. The pastor attends a seminar held by a successful church on how to become a megachurch—a dream

> *We don't have time to sit in board meetings and fight over who is in charge. We have a world to change!*

of his since before he planted this church with a few close friends.

His new "vision" is met with resistance especially from the one elder who works in corporate America. "While we know you to be a man of God, brother, the job of creating vision belongs to the whole eldership, not just the Senior Pastor." Another elder comes back from vacation with an idea gleaned from the church he visited where his daughter and son-in-law are members. His excitement over what he perceives to be the key to moving forward in growth is interpreted by the pastor as dissatisfaction and a growing lack of commitment. Still another elder reminisces over dinner about the glorious days of old and ponders aloud if churches really need to grow after all.

Feeling a need to keep things in line, the pastor reaches for greater control and, in an effort to exert his God-given authority, announces a new initiative from the pulpit without consulting the elders. The next elders' meeting is really the next embers' meeting as members smolder, acknowledging the rightness of the new idea but burning over the wrongness of the way in which things were handled. Eventually, embers turn to flame when, in an entirely different discussion, the pastor suggests that the church considers buying a new computer system. Not immediately recognizing their reaction as stemming from strife over the issue of control and authority, the elders decide to tighten the purse strings and reject the computer idea.

In my travels inside and outside our network of churches, I have seen this type of scenario happen time and again. Sadly, this type of interaction and jockeying for control is far too common in local churches. That which began as life-giving, rewarding, and even fun has become dead, boring, and stressful.

Most churches stuck in non-growth patterns lose people from the periphery but, unfortunately, also from the core. Often, over time, the very ones who made the church what it is, depart, distraught over what they feel it has become, or in some cases, hasn't become. Many times, they leave to join churches which are growing—larger, more vibrant expressions of the body of Christ. These growing churches seem to move along effortlessly. Everything they do seems to work, while making anything work in the non-growth church is a major effort.

These painful endings to long-standing relationships only add to the strife and frustration in churches that are needlessly stuck behind a growth barrier. In some instances, hopelessness and a sense of defeat set in, replacing the youthful, expectant faith of the past with a desire to just hold on and wait for better days.

Everywhere I go, I see the same problems. Pastors are frustrated with their leadership teams, and the leadership teams are frustrated with their pastor. Typically the church is not growing, and the mechanisms required for problem solving have become ensnared in the quagmire of confusion.

Every church goes through certain phases in its journey toward growth, as it pursues the vision of the house. As it grows, the local church encounters certain numerical barriers to growth. C. Peter Wagner has well documented these barriers and widely published the tried and true principles for breaking these barriers. Having helped local churches through these barriers for years, I have noticed that in all churches (but especially in churches built after, what I call, a "New Testament model" or New Apostolic Paradigm), the transition period prior to reaching the growth barrier requires internal change in the unseen mechanisms of the function of the church, namely, in the relationship between the Senior Pastor and the local church leadership team or eldership. If those changes are made, then the church is prepared to address the growth barrier successfully. If the *internal* changes are not made—and most never detect the need for internal restructuring—the church will never make it through the barrier no matter how many *external* changes they make.

Whenever I talk to pastors, it never fails—we always get around to talking about their frustration with trying to bring a vision to life. Whenever I talk to eldership or leadership teams, it never fails—they are struggling, at some point, with the pastor. They all love each other and are committed to the success of the church, but over time something has gone wrong. That "something" is a failure to recognize a transition. And now the tension caused by needed, yet neglected restructuring has affected precious long-term relationships.

On the road to "mega" there are three key stages of leadership structures or configurations and two major transition points. Tension mounts as these transition points are approached. These tension points, interestingly enough, occur at the same point as the major growth barriers. If local church pastors and leaders properly anticipate these transitions and adjust appropriately, stress can be reduced, and leadership teams can work together to experience growth instead of working against each other. In this book you will find tools, proven effective, that will help you pilot the church through these barriers and on into new vistas of church life that are life-giving, rewarding, and even fun once again.

For the record, I am not simply interested in helping churches get larger. I am interested in helping them become healthy from the inside out, so they *can* grow. If the internal structures of the church are not properly aligned, the rest of the church will not function properly either. My passion is to see people released into ministry, not just leaders, but every member in the church. I want to see people becoming who God created them to be and functioning maturely in all their gifts and callings. I want to see the church released into the world, acting as a vehicle for the aggressive advance of the kingdom of God on earth. I want to see the church change the world, and average everyday believers being the ones used by

God to do it! In order for this to happen, the church has to be structured in a way that will best facilitate the development and release of His people. We don't have time to sit in board meetings and fight over who is in charge. We have a world to change!

CHAPTER ONE

THE POWER
OF VISION

I recently asked a group of some thirty young men whom I was training for full-time ministry a question that brought varied and well-thought-out answers. "What is the most important thing to make a church or ministry successful?" While each was convinced his answer was correct, and while most had an eye on a piece of the puzzle for the overall long-term program of local church health, all but three missed the mark. If we have learned one thing from the church growth movement over the years, it is that leadership is the one thing that must be present for growth to occur.

What is the magic of leadership? Why is it so important in taking a church or ministry where God wants it to go? The answer is this: It isn't really leadership itself or even the personality of the leader that moves a church or ministry along, but the natural outworking or application of that leadership gift within the person of the leader. Simply put, it isn't the presence of leadership in an organization that produces movement, but it is what leaders naturally do that produces and sustains momentum. Let me explain.

Leadership always expresses itself in two ways: vision and faith. This is true in the secular and sacred worlds alike. Left alone and placed in charge of anything, leaders will begin to dream about the future and fashion an ideal in their minds that is brighter than the present. At first, the dream is only a dream, distant and unattainable. But over time, as they turn the new vision around and around in their head and heart, a confidence begins to grow that this picture can become a reality.

Soon they begin to share these new thoughts with others who, at first glance recognize the improbability of the new ideal, but at the same time, are strangely drawn toward a belief that the new vision can actually come to pass.

Somehow, they can see what the leader sees. Envisioning what they never saw before and filled with the belief that what they mutually imagine can come to pass, employees or church members begin to work with a calm assurance that the new plan will work, and a new future will be formed. People who formerly came to work to earn a check or came to church to enjoy a service, are now marshaled into a force to accomplish a task, and the business or congregation moves forward as a result.

The leader made this happen, but not by simply being a leader in the midst. This progress occurred because of the natural manifestation of leadership among a people—the expression of vision and faith.

The Formation of Vision

The formation of vision is a solo project. It begins with a dream. Everyone dreams of a better tomorrow—dreaming is easy for most, but turning dreams into an attainable vision is the product of leadership. What is vision anyway? In a Christian context, vision is the ability to see what God wants to do in a given situation. In reference to the local church, vision is the ability to see what God wants to do in and through a group

Fantasies never come to pass because they inherently lack the faith necessary to mobilize one to work effectively, whereas the faith required to create a real vision inspires the visionary and those around to put their best effort forward.

of people. The leader *sees* the future. Vision has everything to do with sight, but not natural sight. Vision is seeing through the eyes of the heart. True vision is far more powerful than natural sight. A leader filled with vision can look beyond the small numbers, financial difficulty, and impossibilities of the present and see, with clarity and passion, the future as if it has already come to pass. For the leader, the problems of the present are temporary inconveniences to be tolerated on the road to what will certainly be a more glorious future. The future is just around the corner and almost in reach. In seeing it, the leader can almost touch it.

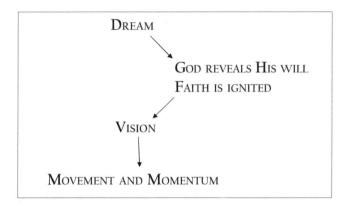

What then is the difference between a vision and a dream? Everything! Most people dream. But a dream without faith is a fantasy. There is nothing wrong with having dream, with meditating on a fantasy about what God *could* do. In fact, all vision is drawn from the well of dreams. The difference is that vision is a statement of what God *will* do. When leaders first conceive of the possibilities for the future, they are like everyone else—dreaming of a better tomorrow. But somewhere along the line, something happens. God begins to impart faith to the leader. The dream begins to mutate and become something more concrete.

As the leader interacts with God over the dream, God imparts faith for the parts of that dream that are according to His will. That faith makes the vision seem so real, so attainable. To those "looking on," the vision seems unreachable, but when leaders speak and share their hearts on the matter, faith becomes like a contagion, and others begin to believe that what formerly seemed impossible can actually come to pass.

Without the element of faith, the vision remains the creation of the human mind—a fantasy. Many people, enamored with a dream, chase it, hoping it will come to pass. But the

Bible says, "*He who works his land will have abundant food, but he who chases fantasies will have his fill of poverty*" (Prov. 28:19). Fantasies never come to pass because they inherently lack the faith necessary to mobilize one to work effectively, whereas the faith required to create a real vision inspires the visionary and those around to put their best effort forward. They work toward what they believe can and will come to pass.

All of this dreaming, praying, believing, and seeing happens in the heart of one person. That is why the formation of vision is a solo project. One person dreams and interacts with God over that dream. God sorts through the ideas contained in the dream, breathing life into some of them, reconstructing the dream into a vision of His formation, all the while imparting faith as He does it. Some believe that this type of faith is actually a gift given to leaders for just this purpose—making them the guardians of a vision from God to the end that God's people are mobilized as a unit into action.

Moses serves as a beautiful example of the singular nature of the formation of vision. When God decided it was time to deliver His people from bondage, He called on one man— Moses. It wasn't that Moses was inherently special—he was simply selected. God gave him specific instructions and commissioned him to lead. Moses anticipated conflict with those among the Israelites who might challenge his authority, but God was undaunted. Moses was to be the man. While Aaron was allowed to stand at Moses' side, it was Moses alone who met God at the bush, and Moses alone who would ascend the mountain for direction.

When Aaron and Miriam challenged Moses as the solo voice of visionary leadership, God responded with sharp criticism of their attitudes. When the sons of Korah put forth that they should have a hand in shaping the course for the Hebrews to follow, the ground actually opened up and swallowed 250 of them! When God wanted to give direction to the people, He called Moses alone to the top of the mountain or into the tent of meeting. It has always been God's pattern to use one leader who would speak for Him in guiding the people into the vision of His destiny for them.

Before Moses, there were Abraham and Noah. After him came Joshua, Samuel, Gideon, and Deborah. They were followed by others: David, Daniel, and Jeremiah, to name a few. Some were quick to step to the fore, while others recoiled from the prospect of solitary leadership, but all were selected by God to cast a vision for the people. Never was the formation of vision the product of a committee, and every attempt at such was met with God's displeasure.

The Threefold Law of Vision

Not only is the formation of vision a solo project, but the function of vision is also in the hands of one leader. Every vision that comes to pass goes through three stages. This is what I call the "Threefold Law of Vision." Nowhere in the Bible is this seen so clearly as in the early ministry of Nehemiah. Having heard of the state of disrepair of the walls surrounding the Holy City in his homeland far away, Nehemiah, the Cupbearer, requested leave of the king to return and rebuild. With his petition granted, and a host of exiles in-tow, Nehemiah returned to Jerusalem to reconstruct necessary ramparts of defense and restore the city's dignity. Consider the following from the narrative:

By night I went out through the Valley Gate toward the Jackal Well and the Dung Gate, examining the walls of Jerusalem, which had been broken down, and its gates, which had been destroyed by fire. Then I moved on toward the Fountain Gate and the King's Pool, but there was not enough room for my mount to get through; so I went up the valley by night, examining the wall. Finally, I turned back and reentered through the Valley Gate. The officials did not know where I had gone or what I was doing, because as yet I had said nothing to the Jews or to the priests or nobles or officials or any others who would be doing the work. **Then** *I said to them, "You see the trouble we are in: Jerusalem lies in ruins, and its gates have been burned with fire. Come, let us rebuild the wall of Jerusalem, and we will no longer be in disgrace." I also told them about the gracious hand of my God upon me and what the king said to me. They replied, "Let us start rebuilding." So they began this good work.* (Neh. 2:13-18, emphasis added).

Notice first, that Nehemiah went alone, at night, to examine the walls. It was not a move of independence, but a desire to first avoid clouding his mind with the opinions of the "committee;" and second, a desire to allow his heart time alone with God to formulate the plan of God's design. No doubt, those initial moments were devastating. He probably asked himself what he had gotten himself into. He didn't need opinions, he needed God! Soon he rehearsed the graciousness of God and encouraged himself. Then he began to "see" what could be. Faith ignited in his heart, and he knew that what he saw in his heart could come to pass, even though what he saw with his eyes so dramatically contradicted that proposition.

Step One: The Law of Articulation

Nehemiah cast the vision to the people. He pointed to the need and suggested a bold solution. He made it so clear, they could see the possibility. I call this first step, the "Law of Articulation." The guardian of the vision has to be able to accurately articulate the vision so that "the many" can see it as one man. Most pastors jump right from step one into attempting to bring the vision to pass. Often they are frustrated by the reluctance of the people to "get on board." Unfortunately, the very nature of vision works against the pastor at this point. Their faith makes the thing seem so doable, so close, that they impatiently reach for its accomplishment and alienates the very ones necessary for its successful implementation.

Step Two: The Law of Unification

Step two is a must. I call it the "Law of Unification." The timing of God is determined by the pace at which the people of God rally around the vision. A lot of factors come into play here—the skill of the leader in articulating the overall vision in terms of doable goals or steps, the health of the body to whom the vision is proposed, and a host of other points of consideration. Notice in the Nehemiah account, "*They* said, '*Let us* start rebuilding.'" The goal of vision is to rally the troops. If that isn't the result, the leader need not waste time in critical thought toward the people. Rather, the leader needs to return to the "mountain" for additional sessions with God.

Step Three: The Law of Mobilization

Finally, once the group buys the vision and makes it their own, the third law, the "Law of Mobilization" comes into play. The people, seeing and believing a vision they had not seen before, step into action. The work of the whole, the force of many, is what brings a vision from being seen with the eyes of one heart, to being seen with the eyes of all in reality.

Three Key Questions

While the formation and function of vision begins in and flows through the life of one, it is clear that others must come into the picture for the second and third law to operate as required. This is where the leadership team comes in. While Nehemiah acted alone in hearing from God, having heard from Him, he immediately shared the vision with those who were leaders in Israel. Moses was chided by his father-in-law for being a one-man-show and not including the leaders God had given him in the process of implementation. Moses alone received the vision, but the people of God were going nowhere without the leaders God had established among them.

In applying these principles to the local church I see a series of questions that must be settled in order to avoid the stress and strain that unnecessarily plagues most leadership teams. If these issues are not settled, we will find ourselves looking a lot like the nation of Israel. We have elders meetings where the Aarons and Miriams, or worse, the rebellious Sons of Korah, reach to take what God has not given them. We attend meetings where Senior Pastor Moses unwisely tries to hold onto what rightly belongs to the leaders God has gathered around him. The questions are three: what, when, and how.

What?

The first question, is "what?" What is God's plan for this house? What is the vision, the mission for which this church has been established by God? The answer to that question, as I have already shared, is given by one person—the Senior Leader. While many others may hear from the Lord in a local church and add to the ideas surrounding the implementation of the vision, the vision itself flows through the one whom God has called to lead them. When Jesus speaks to the seven churches in the second and third chapters of Revelation, while it is clear that the messages are to the entire local church in that particular city, the Lord addresses His comments to the "angel of the church." Most Bible scholars believe that to be the pastor of the church. In speaking "to" the church, He speaks "through" the leader.

When?

Left alone, the idea above is a very dangerous proposition. Sadly, we have seen many abuses of authority in the body of Christ over the years. Fortunately, the "what" question is balanced by two others, the first of which is "when?" When leaders come down from the "mountain," their greatest friend and worst enemy is the vision residing in their heart. Their faith to see the thing come to pass both empowers and deceives them. Faith creates the charisma that draws people to do what they never could before. But faith is very "now" oriented and can produce a drive and an impatience that is unhealthy for local churches.

That is why God has added other leaders—elders in the biblical context—to assist in the implementation of that vision. They are responsible to insure that the steps required to accomplish the grand task are laid out at a pace that the "ewes and lambs" may keep. These are trusted counselors. Understanding their place, they would never restrain the leader from walking in the God-given calling to lead. But they do, in the counsel of multiple elders, help the leader break the plan into workable parts on a reasonable timetable. Wise leaders, while somewhat disappointed that the vision cannot come to pass as fast as they would like, or even as fast as they perceive possible, acknowledge the valuable role of the elders to find the best sense of pace. They know that rushing into implementation too soon can lead to unnecessary failures and turn the people against that which God has given. And without the people, as we have already seen, nothing lasting will happen in bringing the plan to reality.

How?

The third and final question that must be settled is "how?" The Bible clearly instructs us that *"in a multitude of counselors there is safety"* (Prov. 11:14). A vision is a lofty goal, a picture of the future. Those who are natural visionaries themselves, can easily see such a picture and happily work toward it. But the majority of folks are not natural visionaries and need to see the next step—the one right in front of them. While they may lose contact with the overall vision, they easily attend to the task at hand, working to accomplish one goal at a time.

Elders help the leader break the vision into parts that people can manage, and design a plan that produces a string of successes—thus creating unstoppable momentum. The leaders are taken from among the people and feel what the people feel. They are invaluable at this point. Being included in the practical "how" of the vision draws elders/leaders into ownership and releases them to lead among the people. Wise senior pastors who embrace the counsel of the elders in this way, actually multiply themselves among the people. The voice of vision—once spoken by the leader alone—is now spoken on the lips of many, in settings and circles beyond the scope of the influence of one person.

Not Just Theory

In the Introduction, I talked about three stages of leadership structures, transitions, and tension points. The idea is that internal leadership structures will need to change in order for the church to break through the barriers that threaten to hold them back. While these internal structures (namely the way in which senior pastors and leadership teams or elders interrelate) need to undergo adjustment, some things will never change. The "what" of vision will always belong to the Senior Pastor and the "when" and "how" will belong to the Senior Pastor and elders, as partners in leading the church to growth and health.

These ideas are not just theories to me. I have learned by experience, both others'and mine. In my early years, I had plenty of heartache in trying to bring my vision to life. I worked and worked but didn't get anywhere. Now our momentum is seemingly unstoppable. My relationship with the eldership team, and their relationships with each other have changed in keeping with what I have learned over the years. As a result, at the time of this writing, I am pleased to share that there has not been one angry word shared in an elders' meeting in 15 years! Not one! Not one angry word, not one move for control, not one dismissal of a renegade elder! While we are not *nearly* perfect and many times stumble through the process, even in frustration we do it together, all pursuing the same vision, and all confident we are in the place we belong. In the next chapter, I'll share how this can be your experience as well.

CHAPTER TWO

EVERY STAGE
REQUIRES CHANGE

I wish I had known these things when I first started as a
Senior Pastor! I knew that creating and casting vision was
my responsibility, but I had no clue about including the other
parts of the team in the process. I was eager to hear from God
about His plan for us, and so I did just that. I spent lots of time
"on the mountain" seeking God's face and dreaming about
His future for us. No one told me that faith would result from
taking the dream continually before the throne. No one told
me that a real vision would eventually emerge as faith and a
clear picture of God's will co-mingled in my heart. It just
happened. What they did tell me was that I needed to include
the other leaders in the house in creating a plan to bring the
vision to pass. I didn't listen. I had the vision God had given
me. I reasoned that God and I were a majority, and the elders

just needed to get on the wagon and ride. If I needed their help, I would ask them. I was *so* humble.

At 26 years of age, I had stepped into the Senior Pastor role of a 350 member church where I had served as an elder, youth pastor, and associate pastor for three years. I should have known better. These elders and pastors were guys I loved and trusted. We were teammates, most with far more experience than I. They were behind me all the way, and because of that, they believed the vision.

But in believing the vision, they could see straight through the web of deception the vision had spun around me. They tried to speak words of wisdom to me. "Brother, this is all good, but you are trying to go too fast with this. The sheep are not able to keep up with this pace. These are great goals, and I hope every one of them comes to pass, but what plan do you have to bring them to pass?" I didn't listen. I felt I couldn't listen. I didn't know I was supposed to listen. They should be listening to me! I responded by trying to sell the vision harder.

The real trouble was that I didn't know how to relate to the elders. I had been an elder, but now that the table was turned, I couldn't seem to interface with them in a way that brought the best out of them and provided me the help I felt I needed. I was committed to having elders in the church, because the office and function is clearly spelled out in Scripture.

Further, I knew the "one-man-show" to be a dangerous game. So I tried to feel my way along. At first, I included them in everything, but that only bogged me down and drove me crazy. Then I backed up and only included them in key decisions, but the direction and drive of the daily affairs came only from me. This made them feel left out and prompted them to reach for more. Then, I would feel as if they were questioning me. (I am so glad those days are over!) Finally, in frustration, I confided in a member of the pastoral staff who had formerly served as a Senior Pastor himself. "I don't know what to do with the elders! I see them in Scripture, but what we are experiencing cannot be what God had in mind." With the voice of a sage, my trusted friend said to me, "Michael, you are not the leader you one day will be. Right now you must decide how you see the elders functioning in the local church. Are they to be advisors? Are they lay-pastors? Are they overseers? If so, what and how do they oversee? They will take their cue from you."

I learned my first lesson. It was up to me to set the tone and direct the elders as to how they were to relate to the local church and to me as the Senior Pastor. I was clueless as to exactly how to proceed, but I knew for certain that the ball was in my court.

Different Structures, Both Inside and Out

Over time, I began to see that there are various stages in the life and development of a local church. A small church is very much different from a medium-sized church. In the same way, a medium-sized church is very much different from a large church. The real difference is not the size, but in the way the internal functions of the church operate. In fact, size is the least of the differences! Everything about these various-sized churches is different.

Some people think the church that started with just a few families two years ago should and will be the same church ten years from now, with the exception of having more people attending. Not so! Let me illustrate. If there is a change in the schedule when a church is new, a few phone calls will set things right. But that won't work when there are 150 people in the church. How they communicate has to change. As the church grows, how we change and how fast we change needs to adjust with the growth. In the church plant, if the pastor decides the church needs more fellowship, a call today results

In order to cross over into a new stage, leaders must understand what is ahead of them and make the necessary realignments before they expect to move to a new level of growth.

in a church picnic tomorrow. With 150 members, it takes a little more planning. With 2000 members, picnics are not possible at all, but fellowship is still important. Mechanisms that provide for fellowship have to be carefully built into the fabric of the philosophy of ministry, an enterprise not undertaken overnight. The issues all remain the same—fellowship, Bible study, prayer, outreach, assimilation, and communication—but the function of attending to these needs changes as the church goes through various stages of growth.

If the church does not change the way in which they address these and the many other needs and functions of church life, they will actually hinder growth. For example, people may enjoy getting that phone call about the picnic from the pastor, and when the church is small, this is a nice pastoral touch. But as the church grows and people are added, the pastor has a harder time keeping up with everyone. It's harder now to tell those who are "in" from those who are almost "in." In calling those the pastor knows, the pastor leaves out one or two of the families who are on the verge of joining. Now a message is sent that is exactly the opposite of the one intended. While some are being powerfully touched and included, others are being told they are not wanted.

In all likelihood, similar messages are being sent through other channels of ministry to new people. When the new folks stop coming, church members, and unfortunately leaders, often shake their heads and say, "It's a shame those folks just didn't have what it takes to get 'folded in' here." Things have to change for a church to continue growing. I have heard it said that growth brings its own problems. Those problems all have to do with areas in the local church that must be adjusted in order for the church to continue to go forward.

Even when churches do change in the externals of ministry, and most don't (studies show that 75% of Protestant churches in North America have under 150 members), growth will not occur unless the hidden structures are reworked as well. I have visited numbers of local churches who have all the trappings of the megachurch—power point sermons, television screens in the hallways, state-of-the-art websites, etc.—but they still number in the 150 range. Today, folks have the

notion that copying the mega model on the outside will produce mega growth. The real issue isn't just getting the out-
ward trappings in line but readjusting in the inward operations
of leadership. A human will not be able to grow simply by
adding more skin and muscle. Simultaneous with the growth
of soft tissue is the growth of the skeletal structure as well.
Simply put, old ways of operating will keep us in the old
way. If we want to break into the new, new structures will
have to be developed.

Crossing Over into a New Stage

In order to cross over into a new stage, leaders must understand what is ahead of them and make the necessary realignments *before* they expect to move to a new level of growth.
Look into the mechanisms of leadership in the next stage
and build accordingly, in advance of hitting the next barrier
to growth. We will look more deeply into this idea later.
What is important here is that we grasp the notion that we
must build for the next stage prior to reaching it. At this
point, we need to examine the various stages and learn more
about the important characteristics that are common to each.
Look at the chart on page 46. Notice first of all, that we have
already dealt with the questions pertaining to the formation,
function, and implementation of vision.

What isn't addressed is the internal ministry structure of
a church plant. That is because a church plant is like the
"ameba" of church life. All the functions of church life take
place inside one small cell. Everyone in the church is connected to everyone else. Leadership in the church plant is

often in the hands of one who receives input informally from a few trusted mature friends. Usually there is no formal structure. In terms of how ministry happens, a church plant is an "all hands on deck" operation. Anyone and everyone does whatever it takes to move the group forward. As soon as leaders are identified (whether they are elders or not) and responsibilities are doled out, the church plant begins to take on the characteristics of a small church.

In analyzing the various stages of church development, we'll examine three key ideas: 1. how the elders relate to ministry, 2. who actually does the ministry, and 3. how decisions are made.

The Small Church

1. How the Elders Relate to Ministry

In the small church, the elders are the ones who are actually "doing" the ministry. These are the people who have been raised up to help carry the load. They literally take responsibilities from the pastor. As the church grows from the church plant stage and further develops inside the context of the small-sized church, this transfer of responsibility is vital. Ministry is multiplied and people are helped. At the same time, the pastor is released to function in more particular gifting.

It is likely that the eldership team is comprised of the key players of the various functions of ministry in the local church. The worship leader, Sunday School director, finance person, small group leader, and perhaps even the youth leader, among a number of other possible position heads, are probably elders. In this way, the elders are very "hands-on" in ministry. Simply put, they are the ones who do it. If someone needs counsel, it will be an elder who counsels them. Elders are the ones who visit the sick, lead evangelism teams, teach the classes, etc.

2. Who Does the Ministry?

In the beginning, the most mature and capable ones are often those who are designated as elders. In most cases, these are the ones who most qualify to minister in public ways. Often, at least in the early days, there are few others who are able to serve. Even as others are raised up, the elders have also grown in wisdom and competence in ministry, so the people naturally continue to look to them. Consequently, the elders are the ones who actually do the bulk of the ministry needed in a small local church.

3. How Are Decisions Made?

The elders make all the decisions. Not only do they make the big ones—when and where to buy property, who gets hired, etc., but they make small and medium decisions as well. The elders might be the ones who review the curriculum for Sunday School. They will also decide on colors to paint the hall in the nursery area. I was in an elders' meeting where changing the color of the front door was discussed for over one hour!

All the decisions pertaining to the local church, in some way, make it through the agenda of an elders' meeting in a small church. If they don't, and someone begins to call the shots inside the ministry they oversee without including an elder at some point, they are likely to be seen as independent at best, and rebellious at worst.

The Medium Church

1. How Elders Relate to Ministry

Often, after a church breaks through the 100/200 barrier, ministries and competent leaders multiply, so some, if not many, of the oversight responsibilities may now be delegated. It is unreasonable for all these new leaders to be considered elders, so a second tier of leadership begins to informally develop. The pastor and elders sense that accountability is not what it was, and they now feel somewhat out of touch. In the "old days," all the major ministries were represented by the people who served as elders. Now, most of what is done in the church is led by someone else.

Often, elders are then appointed to oversee sections of ministry led by other leaders. One elder might be in charge of all small groups, while another might have oversight of the Sunday School and children's ministries. Someone else oversees music and sound, while another watches after the men's, women's, and singles' fellowships. These elders may not actually attend these functions each week, but they work with the leaders who do. From a leadership perspective, rather than their hands being "on" ministry, their hands are "in" ministry. Rather than doers, they have become overseers.

In order for a church to reach this level of development and growth, more than one pastor is serving on staff. In this stage, it is likely that there will be several full or part-time staff pastors. In most churches, all of these pastors are considered elders. In fact, in most situations, it is considered automatic that a staff pastor is also an elder.

2. Who Does the Ministry?

The people in the church, under the oversight of an elder, are the ones who actually do ministry in the medium-sized church. No doubt, the elders themselves are also involved in the function of touching people, but this is now according to gifting and personal interest and not exclusive to the position of elder. Before, they did everything because they had to. Now that others have been raised up to lead the people, elders are free to minister as individuals in the local church and as regular members, because they are drawn to a particular ministry, not because as elders they are there by position.

3. How Are Decisions Made?

While in a small church, the eldership team makes all decisions together. In the medium church, they make ministry decisions. Sunday School curriculum, formerly chosen by the whole group, is probably now selected by the elder overseeing the children's ministry in consultation with those who serve as leaders in this arena every week. The elders then approve or disapprove the choice—not "hands-on" but "hands-in."

The destination of the annual youth mission trip might be discussed by the elder in oversight with the youth leadership and then presented to the elders as a whole for approval—again, not "hands-on" but "hands-in." The Deacons, or a committee, might deal with colors, for example, but they don't make a final decision until they make a formal or informal presentation to the board of elders.

The Large Church

1. How Elders Relate to Ministry

The large church has multiple staff members. Competent pastors and ministers serve the church in various areas of concentration. The larger the church gets, the more specific these concentrations tend to become. For a church to get to this level, some of its pastors will not serve as part of the eldership team. At this stage, the role of eldership is almost strictly governmental. In fact, as a church moves from small to medium, and medium to large, the ministry role of eldership decreases, and their governmental role proportionately increases. As a consequence of this, the role of elders in a large church is primarily advisory in nature. While the skill of ministry is the quality that sets elders apart in the small church, and the ability to lead in the medium church, it is the wisdom of the elders in the large church that is at a premium.

2. Who Does the Ministry?

The staff in a large church acts almost like an eldership in its relationship to the daily affairs of the church. Things happen way too fast to keep the elders up to date on all the details of daily church life. So the staff works together to take care of the operation of the many ministries in a large church. Pastors and staff oversee these ministries in much the same way elders do in the medium church. Almost all the ministries

TRANSITIONS AND TENSIONS IN GROWTH

Changing Roles and Functions of Elders

Size of Church	Small Church 100/200	Medium Church 100/200	Large Church 700/800
Elders' Relation to the Ministry	• *Do* the ministry • Hands *on*	• *Over* the ministry • Hands *in*	• *Advise* the ministry
Who Does the Ministry	• The Elders (There may be no one else to help—must do it themselves.)	• The Elders are over the ministry. • People do the ministry. (Elders organize and lead groups of people to perform the ministry.)	• The staff is over the ministry. • The people do the ministry. (Elders are more removed and more like a Board of Directors—may not even be aware of all that is going on ministry-wise. Elders deal only with the big matters.)
Decision-Making	• Elders make all the decisions.	• Elders make ministry decisions.	• Elders make policy decisions.

are actually run by church members. These people oversee the other members in the church who serve alongside them.

Churches slice the pie in different ways. Some divide their church into districts and place all the functions of the church under the pastor who oversees that particular district—benevolence, cell groups, counseling, etc. Other churches adopt a departmental model and place pastors as specialists over certain operations of the church—cell groups, education, worship and fine arts, missions, etc. Still others use a combination, but all end up seeing their pastoral staff primarily as equippers, overseeing and releasing people into ministry—leading leaders. As a church grows larger, there is no way to hire enough staff to actually do all of the ministry. Members, overseen by members, under the care of a staff pastor are the primary ministers.

3. How are Decisions Made?

It is extremely unwise to attempt to turn a large ship too fast. In fact, leaders who are prone to this style of leadership are probably not going to be able to lead a church to this point. That is not to say that large churches are inflexible. Since most of the daily decisions are made by the staff, large churches can function just as fluidly as any medium-sized church, even more fluidly in some cases. Rather than wait for decisions to be made at weekly elders' meetings, large churches can make decisions on a daily basis. In fact, to maintain momentum, they have to.

The elders in a large church concern themselves with policy decisions. In order to make daily decisions, the staff needs clear direction concerning what they can and cannot do, and the kinds of decisions they can and cannot make. Policies give direction and provide "tracks" upon which the staff may run. Policies are designed to facilitate the vision in the local church and give practical direction to the members who oversee and serve in the various functions of church life. "He who pays the piper, calls the tune." So those who frame the budget, decide the direction of the church. Final approval of the financial direction comes from those whose mission is not strictly defined in terms of a district or some specialized area of ministry, but by those whose eyes are on the health of the church as a whole, and whose passion is the pursuit of the vision of the house. In the end, the elders are those who "call the tune."

What Does Not Change

In all three stages, one thing never changes—the roles of the Senior Pastor and the elders in relation to the vision. The Senior Pastor is always responsible for the "what." Both the pastor and the elders work together to formulate the "when" and "how."

That which I have shared above is in no way to be considered exhaustive in reference to the role of elders in the local church. We simply looked at how they function in relationship to three issues at various levels in the development of the local church. Our purpose in so doing was to provide insight into the various stages, so leaders can prepare properly for the transitions required to move from one stage to another. Between each stage is a seemingly impenetrable barrier, the nature of which is the subject of the next chapter.

CHAPTER THREE

CHURCH GROWTH DYNAMICS AND BARRIERS

For a long time, the chart on page 46 had no numbers on it at all. I simply defined small, medium, and large churches in terms of the dynamics I saw operating within them. Actually, the chart was first put to paper (on a napkin to be exact) in an effort to describe to the pastor of a church that was bumping up against the 100/200 barrier, why he and certain members of his leadership team were having conflicts. (I carried that same napkin all over the country, working with churches until one of my pastor friends put it into a form akin to what you see in this book.)

Everywhere I went, pastors and leaders asked me to define small, medium, and large by assigning a numerical designation to each. I strongly resisted, because I felt the key to progress was not in gauging how well a church was doing relative to a static numerical standard, but how they were progressing in modifying their internal structures to allow for the continued development of the church as it grew.

I had long studied church growth and considered C. Peter Wagner and others to be gifts to the body of Christ in providing helpful tools and invaluable insight into the dynamics of growth in the local church. My reluctance to put numbers on the chart had nothing to do with rejecting the ideas I had learned. Indeed, when we were approaching 2000 members, our local church hosted Dr. Wagner and his seminar on breaking the 100/200 barrier, for the purpose of strengthening the local churches in our city and furthering apostolic networking. I believed what I had heard. My reluctance had more to do with the doubts I had concerning the universal application of what I had discovered. I wanted to look into the workings of more churches before I assigned numbers to the transition points. Over time I became convinced that the transition points I had seen in church after church directly corresponded to the barriers outlined by church growth experts.

So, what are these barriers and how do they work? First, let me hasten to say that I am no expert here. All that I share on this point I have learned from those who truly are the experts. Also, I am not a theoretician; I am a practitioner, so I have applied these ideas in our own local church and shared them with a host of others, with excellent results. These barriers are real, and the way over is tried and true. Many have gone before you. It is impractical for me, at this point, to tell you to put down this book and attend a seminar or read certain pages in a number of books. I will then, attempt to articulate what I have learned about these barriers from study and practical experience.

While there are numerous barriers to growth, most local churches need only concern themselves with two: the 100/200 barrier and the 700/800 barrier. In both cases the numbers have to do with how many active members a church has. Some define this in terms of how many people actually attend the church. Others concentrate on how many adult members a church has. I like to use the term "active" members. Many churches add people to the roles and remove them only upon death, or when former constituents request a transfer of membership to another church. Other churches may purge their roles annually by a variety of methods. Those who remain after the purge are considered the members of the church.

An "active" member in my view is one who can be counted upon to participate in some way in the life of the church. These people regularly give, participate in a small group, or attend weekly services at least once or twice a month. They see themselves as attached to a local church (perhaps not as tightly as the pastor would like) in a living, organic way, not just as a name on the roll.

Once a church hits the range of having 100/200 or 700/800 active members, they have reached a barrier to growth.

The 100/200 Barrier

What makes a small church successful is what will eventually stop its growth. Everyone in the small church knows everyone else. This creates a tight community composed largely of the kind of people who "we like," people who are "like us." This makes fellowship close and builds a family-type atmosphere. Small churches, without realizing it, intuitively resist growth at a certain point, since continued growth threatens the closeness they so enjoy. After a certain number of relationships, there just isn't any room for more. Folks

> *At every level, barrier-breaking begins in the brain. First, the pastor must look ahead and anticipate that change is required.*

cannot remember everyone's name but somehow feel they should. Not knowing everyone, and the underlying guilt that says we should, produces an awkwardness that actually pushes others away. Those who are "in" are in, and those who are "out" are not likely to break in without a tremendous amount of tenacity. Small churches fear that growing might destroy the family they have become.

There are all sorts of unwritten rules—ways things are done and not done in a small church. In the old days, we called ourselves "Mannanites" since the name of our church is Manna Church. People who came were not considered one of us until they had mastered all the hidden rules. No one actually said this, and there wasn't a secret book of rules in some locked drawer. Every local church has a hidden code of do's and don'ts that are learned over time. Knowledge of these is what separates newcomers from the real members, no matter whose name is on the rolls. While no one wants to admit it, the unwritten rules game is a really a control game—a way small churches protect what they worked so hard to build.

Everyone in the small church connects to the pastor, as shown in the diagram below. But one person can only effectively oversee so many others. Some have speculated this to be the main reason churches face a barrier at 100 to 200 active members. From a sociological perspective, a single pastor has reached the limit at this number. This is what some call the Shepherd Model. While there are other respected leaders in the church, the members look to the pastor as the "go-to" person. The pastor is the final say on all matters pertaining to

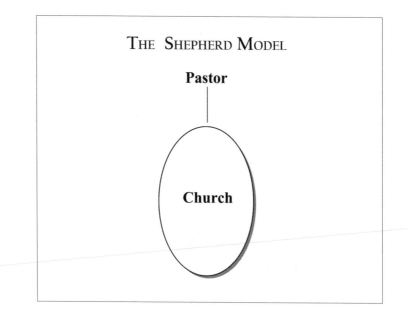

THE SHEPHERD MODEL

Pastor

Church

church life. As the church reaches 200 active members, the phone rings off the hook. The poor pastor becomes exhausted just thinking about the prospect of growing larger.

For a church to break through the 100/200 barrier, at least three things need to happen:

1. The people must accept the fact that they will not be able to know everyone in the church. This does not mean that they will have to lose a sense of family, but it does mean they will have to learn to experience it in other ways. Properly done, this barrier can be broken without destroying the great fellowship members have been enjoying. New circles of fellowship will have to be developed, and even multiplied, to prompt continued growth.

2. The people will have to become inclusive of others, and unwritten rules will have to be supplanted with clear methods of communication. In order for this to occur, new space will have to be created in the hearts of folks for new people. Surprisingly enough, this is more a structural concern than a relational one. You can't make people want more relationships when they already feel full. New internal structures will create opportunities for more people to plug in.

3. The pastor will have to switch from a Shepherd Model to a Rancher Model. Notice in the Rancher Model diagram on the following page that there is more than one circle. This does not mean that there is more than one church meeting in the same location. Nor does it mean that the church has actually split into two. It does mean that another leader

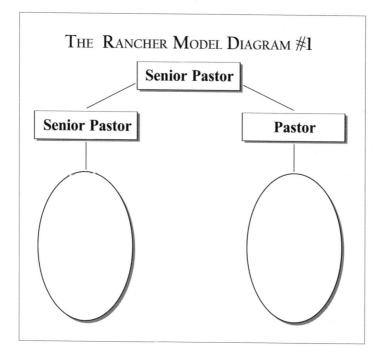

has been raised up to whom people can connect as another "go-to" person. In this leader's sphere of responsibility, that person is the final answer. This leader has the authority to act and lead as a delegated authority of the Senior Pastor.

I have talked with pastors who say, "I have this really great Youth Pastor (or Music Minister or Associate) on staff, so we must already be in the Rancher mode!" That is not necessarily so. The real question is, do folks look to that staff member as a youth expert, or another associate as their pastor? Do they recognize that person as another leader in the house or as the Senior Pastor's junior partner in ministry? Are they confident seeking that person's counsel on personal matters? In short, is there a good portion of the church "connected" to someone other than the Senior Pastor? This idea scares many pastors, but it is essential for this to happen in order for the church to grow. Depending on the types of structures established in the church, a church which has hit a plateau at 180 active members because their circle was full, now may have 100 in one circle and 80 in another, with plenty of room to grow in both (as depicted in the following diagram)!

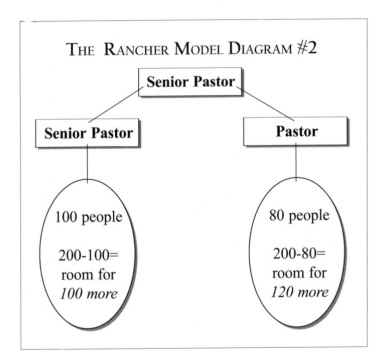

To continue to add growth, all the church has to do is add more circles (as depicted in Rancher Model Diagram #3). It is obvious by now, that adding more circles means adding more leaders. Usually these leaders will be paid members of

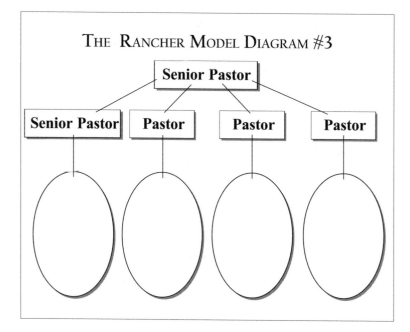

THE RANCHER MODEL DIAGRAM #3

Senior Pastor

Senior Pastor | Pastor | Pastor | Pastor

the pastoral staff, although in a smaller church a strong elder can sometimes function in this role, but this is rare. And even then, as the church grows, paid staff will have to be brought on.

It is my opinion that moving from the Shepherd Model to the Rancher Model is the most important aspect of breaking the 100/200 barrier. In fact, I believe that this infrastructural adjustment is all that is needed to facilitate the changes in the people outlined in the Rancher Model Diagrams #1 and #2 as shown above. When new circles of fellowship are created that are sized to allow for others to join, and more proactive communication processes are implemented, people (who are like sheep) will naturally follow. I am not taking a low view of the people of God; my contention is that it is easier to create new structures than to try to make people ignore the socio-logical laws that tend to govern human behavior. When the church was moving toward the 100/200 barrier, people were added and accepted into the fellowship of the church. In the early days, there was a feeling that there is always room for more. The goal of shifting to the Rancher model is to allow for that dynamic to occur once again.

The First Shift: The Pastor

The leadership structures in the church are then the ones that must undergo the most drastic change in order for this barrier to be broken. The first shift that must occur is in the mind of the pastor. The pastor must embrace the idea of sharing lead-ership and ministry with others. This is a frightening prospect to many. Many pastors are fed emotionally by having all the people look solely to them. They like being the ones who visit the newcomers in their homes and the members in the hospital. They like doing all the counseling and could not bear to be out of the loop in some situation in the life of a parishioner. Unfortunately, pastors who cannot make this mental jump will not be able to lead their churches to make the jump over this first and greatest barrier.

The Second Shift: The Eldership

The second shift that must occur is in the minds and hearts of the eldership. New leaders are going to have to be brought into ministry. That means that the elders can no longer be the ones who do all the meaningful tasks. A second tier of leader-ship must be developed, so responsibility and authority must be delegated. This is crucial. I find that most bottlenecks to growth happen right here in the interaction between the pastor and the elders or between the elders themselves. We'll discuss this in detail in Chapter Five, but I have found very few eldership/leadership teams where all the members were functioning as they should according to their stage of growth. Trouble is always the result, and the church suffers as a consequence.

Elders in the small church often struggle at two main points: 1. they do not want to give up what they perceive to be the control of the church to others who they esteem to be less competent than they, and 2. they fear the growing authority of the pastor. As the church becomes increasingly larger, the role of the Senior Pastor becomes less of a ministry position and more of a leadership position. The more the pastor delegates to others the greater the pastor's authority becomes in the church and the people both feel and respond to that. Elders who have to make all the decisions, and who keep their hands on all the ministry (thus controlling it), and who seek to limit the pastor's authority will not be able to lead the church through this barrier.

The Third Shift: The Congregation

The final shift that must occur is in the minds of the congregation. People want to be led and fed. As long as those two things are happening, they will follow a leader wherever the leader takes them. Personally, I think the people of God as a whole, want to grow, want to love God more, want to learn His ways and become like Him. When leaders sneeze, the sheep catch cold. Everything that happens in the leadership is magnified among the people. Leaders—myself included—

tend to blame the people, when the lack is often really found in our failure as leaders to clearly lead or feed along the way. It isn't enough to simply lead; sheep must be fed as they travel along the course the vision dictates. Sheep don't eat well when they feel insecure.

As pastors lead toward change, the people must be fed with the truths that create an understanding of the need for that change. People are asking, "Why are we doing this? Where are we going? How will this make me a better Christian? How will this increase my opportunities to serve the Lord?" Properly led and fed, they will follow. The people in the large church are no better than the people in smaller churches. It really isn't about the people. It is all about how leaders lead and feed the flock as they structure themselves for growth.

The 700/800 Barrier

We had been stuck at about 800 for over one year. We would break over that mark but then drop back beneath it. I had heard there was a wall to growth around this point but arrogantly thought we could ignore it and just break right through; however, ignoring was no longer possible. Personally, it was taking its toll on me. It is amazing that as every barrier is approached, the Senior Pastor feels it first. That is because the greatest change will have to come in the Senior Pastor in order for growth to continue. Pressure and stress are great motivators to increase knowledge! That is, in fact, one of the reasons this book is being written. I have a burden to help pastors anticipate and make the required adjustments before they hit "the wall."

I asked the Administrator to order a workbook/manual I found in a church growth resource catalog on breaking the 800 barrier. When it came, I was like a little kid and immediately began rifling through it on my way from the administration office into my own. I saw one diagram, closed the book and never picked it up again. I knew exactly what to do. Breaking the 700/800 barrier follows the same dynamics as the 100/200 barrier, but on a "macro" scale.

To break through 200, the church has to restructure from one swollen fellowship circle to multiple circles, allowing more space for people to connect. It has everything to do with people making connections. But as circles increase, so do the management responsibilities of the Senior Leader. Consequently, the elders' meetings increase in length and fre-

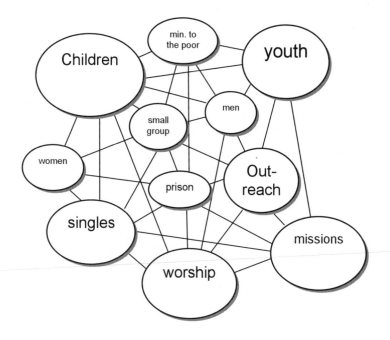

quency to keep up with all the ministry demands. Decisions simply have to be made.

Managing a church like this can be very cumbersome, and things tend to fall through the cracks. Planning can also be a nightmare—cumbersome and complicated. One ministry, for instance, might schedule an event on the same night as another. Since the church is not small, neither are these groups, rendering last minute changes nearly impossible, if not overwhelmingly unprofessional. As the diagram on the previous page suggests, increasing fellowship circles has allowed for more growth, but created a crisis of leadership that is now threatening to strangle the very growth it created.

What is needed is a restructuring of leadership to form circles of circles. Another layer of leadership must be established, this time among the paid staff, to whom new levels of authority and responsibility must be delegated. There are a variety of ways to do this. In a departmental church, circles may be grouped into macro departments where a number of pastors work under the leadership of another pastor who is empowered to run that section of the church.

Since our church is a cell church, we broke the county into three districts and grouped cell groups under each according to categories—circles of circles. We set in a Senior Associate to oversee the daily affairs of the church, since my responsibilities outside the church (apostolic network duties, missions, overseeing churches we had planted) had increased.

As the church increased, we designated a fourth circle comprised of singles and youth cells (diagrams of these are on the following two pages). As medium-sized churches add circles to facilitate continued growth, so large churches add circles of circles to do the same.

THE 700/800 BARRIER DIAGRAM #1

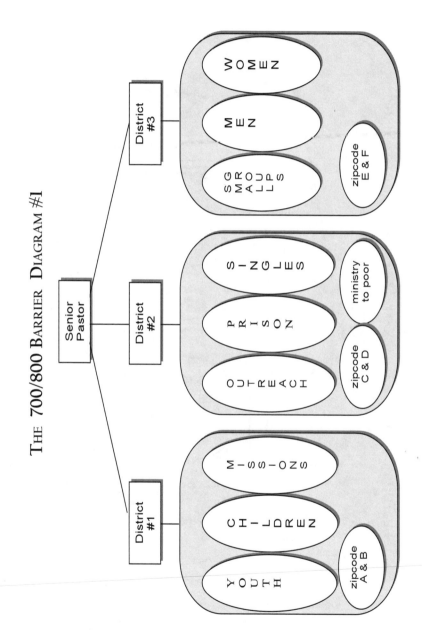

THE 700/800 BARRIER DIAGRAM #2 -- WITH YOUTH & SINGLES

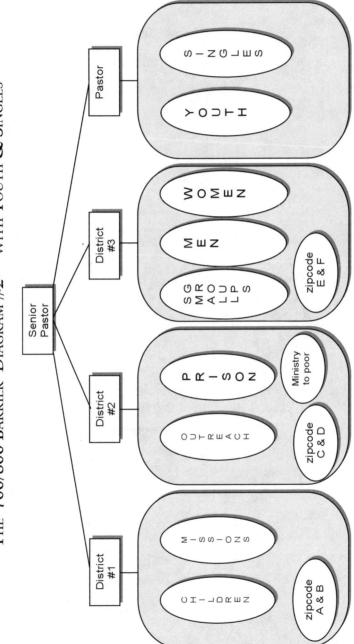

An Adjustment in the Elders

In order to break this barrier, two other crucial adjustments had to be made. The elders had to relinquish control of certain aspects of leadership to the staff. In our situation, all the District Pastors are elders, but the five other pastors are not. If all the pastors are elders, then there really is no difference between an elder and a pastor in terms of the function of government. The elders, therefore, would still have their hands in the daily operations of the church with the exception of those who were not paid. The Senior Pastor would then be forced to decide between keeping the operations of government functioning like a medium-sized church or only having paid elders. First, there is a conflict of interest problem in the latter scenario. Second, there would be no functional elders governing the local church, only fivefold type leaders (see Ephesians 4:11). The New Testament clearly calls for elders in every church (see Acts 14:23) .

An Adjustment in the Pastoral Staff

The second crucial adjustment that had to be made, was that the staff, particularly those at the District tier, had to be empowered to lead at a new level. Each District Pastor was set up to function basically like a church within a church. (Just as the circles in the medium church allow for more people to make connections, so in the large church the grouping of circles under one leader allows for more circles to be created. When the management of a district gets to be too much for one District Pastor, or when that district presses in on the 800 barrier, we simply create more districts.) The entire pastoral staff as a unit was also empowered to engage in creating a yearly calendar to facilitate the pursuit of the vision and create corresponding provisional budgets. Final approval of the budget is in the hands of the eldership, since their focus is on the big picture and not one district or aspect of church life.

Once all these pieces were in place, and the church was gently led along, we sailed right past the 800 mark. The momentum was awesome! At that point, I became even more passionate about the fact that infrastructure, particularly the relationship of the Senior Pastor and the other staff pastors to the eldership, was fundamental to breaking growth barriers.

The Key

The key to breaking both of these barriers is not so much "how" but "why." There are hidden dynamics at work that must be appreciated and can be anticipated. Understanding them enables us to be creative in developing the mechanisms necessary to break through. All the principles are the same; however, the outworking might be different in each context. Things may look one way in one church and a different way in another, even though both applied the same principles.

At every level, barrier-breaking begins in the brain. First, the pastor must look ahead and anticipate that change is required. Second, the pastor must imagine how the church at the next level functions and how it is structured, then must lead the leadership team around to see the same thing. Third, the pastor must begin to formulate a plan to rebuild the infrastructure of the church to fit the newly envisioned model. As the pastor and the elders adjust their functioning relationship, growth will naturally occur. Finally, step by step, the church needs to be led and fed as changes are implemented.

Tension mounts as churches approach a growth barrier. In order to "make the jump" to the next level, certain internal operations must be adjusted. In the next chapter, I will give some practical suggestions on how to make the necessary changes to go over the top.

CHAPTER FOUR

TENSION POINTS
PRODUCED BY
GROWTH BARRIERS

It is much easier to pastor a church with 350 active members than it is a church of 200. By the same token, leading a church of 1500 is infinitely easier than leading a church of 800. Numbers aren't really the issue. As I have already said, the key to leading a church to growth is found in the leader's ability to make the necessary changes to the internal structures of a church in order to facilitate that growth. Those internal changes primarily concern how the elders, senior pastor, and staff relate together—who does the ministry and how decisions are made.

What makes leading a church of 200 more difficult than leading a church of say 400, is simply this: A church of 200 active members arrived at that plateau by developing a certain methodology of ministry and a governmental infrastructure that fueled their growth to this point. As they approach 100/200 active members (a known growth barrier), the methodology and infrastructure employed has run its course of usefulness. This didn't happen overnight. Gradually, the old methods and the infrastructural design began failing to produce the same results as in the earlier days when the church was smaller. In fact, some of these methods and structure began "getting in the way" of growth, as the church approached this dreaded barrier. The same dynamic is at work in a church that has bumped up against the wall of 700/800.

The Developing Tension

Why is leading a church of 300/400 easier than leading a church of 200? Why is leading a church over 1000 easier than leading a church of 800? Tension. The barrier actually creates tension and makes leading and managing a church approaching or parked at that barrier more difficult to lead. Look at the chart on page 46. Notice the line dividing the small church from the medium church, and the line dividing the medium church from the large. These lines are designated 100/200 and 700/800 respectively, indicating the presence of a church growth barrier.

The mechanisms employed to get a church to this threshold will never help them across it. In fact, the closer a church gets to the growth wall ahead, the more tension develops. And that tension is actually caused by the breakdown of the very mechanisms that once worked so effectively to get them to this place.

To illustrate the point, in a small church, the elders "do" the ministry and make all the decisions. When the church is under 100, this makes for pleasant Kingdom activity. But as a church grows toward 200 there are more people to counsel, comfort, and correct. Getting home from church becomes a task all in itself. Decisions demand to be made, so elders' meetings creep past the time limit set in the days when the church was a manageable 100.

Getting home late after church increases tension in the home as do late arrivals from the weekly elders' gathering. Tension naturally increases as the numbers of people who require ministry exceed the limits of the ability of those who minister. Older and less needy members feel neglected. New ministries must be created to keep up with the demand for more pastoral care and to maximize the opportunities presented by the gifting and interests of new and maturing people.

It is not uncommon for an elder or two to step down during this period. Feeling pressure at home, pressure at work, and pressure at church, they request a break. What does that do to the others on the eldership team? With the departure of the resting friend, the work load only increases. Elders sometimes begin to question the management style of the senior pastor: "Is it really necessary to meet for three hours every week? Perhaps you could do a little more by way of preparation for these meetings!"

At times, elders develop stress among themselves: "Do you really have to ask 45 questions about every decision we make?" A change in structure will change everything and take them over the very barrier that is causing the tension

and has made life at 200 miserable. Again, while the dynamics are different, tension caused by outdated structures is the
reason for stress at 700/800 as well.

As was stated earlier, small, medium, and large churches
are completely different from each other. A medium church is
not a small church with more members. Nor is a large church
simply a medium church with a greater attendance. All are
churches, true, but it would be best to think of them as various
species in one family. They are simply not the same. It is
important, then, to understand the dynamics involved in the
church at the next level in order to take the church to that
place.

> *Growing a church is never about
> simply increasing numbers.
> Growing a church is about
> emptying hell and filling up
> heaven. It is about making room
> for harvesters and harvest alike.*

A church that has hit a growth barrier (100/200 or 700/
800) has only three choices: 1. divide the congregation into
multiple congregations and plant new churches, 2. stay the
way they are and plateau at this barrier (in most cases, they
will develop an oscillating pattern of growth and decline with
the barrier being the ceiling of growth), or 3. change and grow
on into the next phase of development. The key word is change;

they cannot break through a growth barrier and remain the way they are. They must change.

Change is not an event. Change is a process. I have seen more than one zealous pastor, filled with vision that is truly from God, turn the ship too quickly, spilling people over the side. The initiative designed to promote growth and build momentum actually hindered both. In such cases, unwise leaders and core members shake off the setback by decrying the lost congregants as those who didn't "want to go on with God." In reality, the loss is a result of leadership that was not patient and deliberate in the introduction of change to the church. The larger the ship, the slower the turn. The church is no longer the little motorized skiff that once met in the living room. You cannot steer 200 the way you steered 50. Turning the ship at 800 the way you turned her at 200 is a great way to "grow" the church to 600!

Few people readily and happily embrace change. Most, in fact, resist it. Over time, the majority of people will "get on board," but there will always be a few who forever speak of the old days as better than the present. Ignore the latter, but you can never get where God has called you to go without the former. Those who immediately accept the new initiative deceive you into thinking that now is the time to aggressively advance. They love change; change is exciting in their view. For them, the future is now. But in the long run they aren't normally "builders." Those who always live in the past will likely never be won. If you wait for all of them to get in the game, the crowd will be gone before the whistle finally blows.

The true builders in the church are the ones who are in the middle group—the ones who will eventually get on board.

These are the ones you have to reach. But how? Every leader navigating the church over a growth barrier needs to address three issues—the problem, the paradigm, and the personnel—each on two levels—elders and people. I will address these issues as they specifically relate to 100/200 and 700/800 walls respectively.

100/200 Barrier

1. The Problem—"We have reached a barrier to our growth. We must change to keep growing."

A. The Elders

It won't take much to convince the elders that change is needed. They have been living with a growing tension for some time prior to reaching the wall of 200. It is the reason for change, and the type of change that they are likely to resist.

The idea that growth barriers exist is not in the Bible. No Sunday School curriculum that I know of ever mentions the idea. Unfortunately, most pastors have never educated the leaders on the topic. Consequently, the idea has never even been batted around in an elders' meeting. The elders must be instructed. Expose the leaders to some material written by C. Peter Wagner. Dare I suggest? Distribute this book among them and discuss it together. Do whatever you have to do, but educate the elders in advance of initiating any change.

In addition to the fact that most people want to be wanted, the power and prestige of being the conduits through whom all decisions and ministry flows is intoxicating. The change you are calling for, as indicated by the chart on page 46, is for the elders to include others in the flow of ministry, delegating responsibility and the corresponding authority. Many are threatened by this and will resist at first. Wise pastors must help elders see that they are not being replaced. They are, in fact, being taken "up" not "down" since they will actually be "over" those doing the ministry.

B. The People

The average church member does not care in the least about church growth barriers. Whole sermons on the subject are not likely to be met with enthusiasm. In fact, I have found, sadly, that most church members are not convinced the church needs to grow. Therefore, any call for sacrifice to facilitate growth will probably be resisted. Instead, the pastor should concentrate on creating an understanding that the church *should* grow, and further, that its growth will *actually benefit* the average believer! C. Peter Wagner's *Leading Your Church to Growth* (Regal Books) and *Your Church Can Grow* (Regal Books) are wonderful resources and contain loads of great material for constructing messages that will speak to this issue.

Above all, seek to destroy all non-growth thinking. Get it out of the church and stand guard at the door so it can never creep back in. Why? Because growing a church is never about simply increasing numbers. Growing a church is about emptying hell and filling up heaven. It is about making room for harvesters and harvest alike. Who would turn someone away from the table of life? No true believer would actively seek to run the lost away from the table but by camping on the underside of a growth barrier, churches passively reject displaced believers and the lost everyday.

I remember a time when the church was busting at the seams, and it was evident that a new building was in our future. The inconvenience of standing through services hoping to find a seat and patrolling the lot for a parking place was causing the patience of folks to wear thin. On top of that was the obvious sacrifice that goes along with funding new construction and putting up with the mess of the physical plant. These people embraced growth and were enthusiastic proponents of our aggressive evangelistic thrust, but I sensed it was time for another dose of Kingdom reality. In a sermon I brought up the thought that no one would dare put into words. I hypothetically proposed, with no small hint of sarcasm, that perhaps we had grown enough; perhaps we should plan to taper off. I suggested we put a sign on the door telling newcomers that we didn't want them.

In the case of believers, we were only depriving them of fellowship, a fellowship we enjoy; but in the case of the unbelievers, we were depriving them of a chance to hear the gospel and come to Christ for salvation. In reference to the latter, I proposed it would be more accurate, in the case of the unbelievers, for us to post a sign that simply said, "Go to Hell!" since our exclusion of them from our services would amount to the same.

Furthermore, I pointed out that we already had a problem with too many people so we would actually need to empty some of our services of the folks who were already in our midst. If the church has become too big, then some obviously need to go! "Perhaps we should make a committee and get rid of those we don't like. What happens if you don't get picked for the committee but are chosen to be among those asked to leave? Would you still feel the church was too big?" To keep the story in context, we were experiencing extreme conditions, and these folks had been under 15 years of teaching on why it is best for them that the church continue growing. By the time the ruse was up, everyone in the place could see the obvious; we had to do whatever necessary to make room for all those whom God would bring our way. We built the building without debt.

2. The Paradigm—The Role of the Elders Will Have to Change.

A. The Elders

As indicated in the chart on page 46, in order for a church to get beyond the 100/200 mark, the internal relationship of elders to ministry must undergo adjustment. First, the elders need to recognize that in letting go of ministry, they are not letting go of their role or authority in the church. The chief function of the eldership is ruling, and the calling on every believer is to ministry. Elders aren't losing anything in releasing ministry and an appropriate amount of authority over that ministry to people. Their role is the same—to rule over. In fact, their role has increased, since that over which they have rule has increased.

Second, elders must resist the temptation to micromanage ministry. As noted earlier, in the small church, elders make all the decisions. Now they must allow for some decisions to be made at the ministry level. They must empower people to lead in their designated sphere of responsibility. Certainly there are limits that are organic in nature, and as such cannot be set forth in this book as applicable in all situations.

An illustration here, however, is in order. A new children's ministry director will likely need more guidance than one who has been functioning for years. The new director might, for instance, need help in choosing curriculum. In fact, the elders may decide to choose it for her/him. But in the case of a person who has years of experience, he/she may be given the authority to change curriculum and even set the annual children's budget. A children's ministry director with years of experience but little wisdom or lots of "attitude," on the other hand, may be very limited in the types of decisions he/she is allowed to make. The idea of delegating responsibility and authority is very organic; but the point is, that in order for the church to grow and people to mature, elders must shift from doing ministry to being over ministry, from "hands-on" to "hands-in."

B. The People

When the church is smaller, the pastor is looking for volunteers. In the medium church, the pastor is looking for leaders. There is simply too much for the elders to do; other leaders must come forward. I have often heard pastors say they don't have any leaders. I believe the real problem is not a lack of leadership on the part of the people, but a lack of perception on the part of the pastor.

I heard Tommy Barnett, pastor of the huge First Assembly of God in Phoenix, Arizona, say that "All you need to reach your city is already in your house (church)." That statement changed my life. Rather than waiting for God to bring great people into the church, I began to look for the great people already in the church.

Some say that leaders are born, not made. No matter what you read on leadership, let me emphatically state that most leaders are "made" not born. Leaders "become;" they don't appear. In fact, the best leaders are the ones you raise up yourself, right in the house—not the ones who come to you from the outside. The leaders trained from within hold your values as non-negotiables. Your philosophy of ministry is already inculcated into the fabric of their leadership style. They love and follow you, because you brought them into their destiny. Leaders brought in from the outside have to be engrafted into the vision of the house and trained in your values and philosophy of ministry before they can be fully released.

"But they aren't ready!" I have heard pastor after pastor (all of whom pastor churches under 200) make that statement. The truth is no one is truly ready for the next step in life. You weren't ready for marriage. You thought you were until the first big blowup. You weren't ready for children, although you thought you knew everything about kids. You judged all your friends who had kids as failures, until you had a couple of children. You weren't ready for ministry either, although as a senior in Bible College you knew the church you planted would break a thousand in the first few years.

No one is ready! So what are you waiting for? Put people in ministry! Don't be foolish or hasty, but look at people through the eyes of faith.

In the thousands of appointments I have made over the years, I have seldom heard others applaud my choice with "He is the man!" Instead, the vast majority of my choices have been made in the face of mild opposition. "Can she really do it?" "I'm not sure about him." "She isn't ready." "You might be setting him up for failure."

Interestingly, even those I have appointed to leadership in opposition to others opinions, have often been among those voicing opposition to the new ones coming along. Believe more for others than they do for themselves, and you will always be successful. Those you raise up will propel you to success.

3. The Personnel – We must move from the "Shepherd Model" to the "Rancher Model."

A. The Elders

The elders are the example-setters in the church; people naturally look to them since they are leaders. As noted earlier, for a church to break the 100/200 barrier, it must switch from the "Shepherd Model" to the "Rancher Model." A second full-time pastor must be brought on staff, or at least (as a temporary measure), an elder functioning as an associate must be raised up. This "Second" can't just be a good person who is cheap (inexpensive to hire) and happens to be at hand. This person has to be the kind of person to whom people can go as a "buck stop" person—a person who can make a final decision.

When this person visits, those in the hospital feel visited and are not looking for the Senior Pastor to come. They feel the pastor visited them. When that person counsels, the folks are satisfied that they have been competently counseled. Obviously, it is imperative that people have confidence in this "Second" if the church is to go forward. Elders need to take the lead in this, intentionally getting behind the Associate and following that person as they would the Senior Pastor. How the elders respond to this person, will dictate how the people will respond.

B. The People

I suppose the most foolish thing the Senior Pastor could do in shifting from a "Shepherd Model" to the "Rancher Model" is ask the people for their opinion on who the next staff member should be. A vote on this issue is a promise of divided loyalty. A pastor can't herd the people over the 100/200 barrier—they must be led. As the pastor must prepare the people to change and make room for growth, so the pastor must prepare them to receive the next staff member. In advance of hiring the new person, tell the people there is a new person coming. Describe the position and tactfully tell the people how you see them relating to the one who fills the new position. As you outline the job description to the people, explain how you, as the Senior Pastor, will also follow this new person in the areas in which you delegate responsibility.

I am not in any way advocating coequal pastoral authority in the church. But when the one who is "over" is secure enough to come "under" in certain areas, it pushes up the subordinate in the eyes of the people to new levels of respect, establishing the subordinate's authority in the house, thus making the whole church stronger. I would never bring this person into the position gradually, hoping the people will embrace the new Associate Pastor. That idea screams that you lack confidence either in the person or in the process of breaking this barrier. Either way, you lose. Do your homework. Win the elders' wholehearted support. Prepare the people. Bring on the Associate Pastor. Shift to the "Rancher Model." Break this barrier!

700/800 Barrier

1. The Problem—"We have reached a barrier to our growth. We must change to keep growing."

A. The Elders

At the 100/200 level the elders are among the first to experience tension as that barrier is approached. At the 700/800 mark, the pastor first, and then the pastoral staff, are the ones who feel the pressure. The elders are likely unaware that this barrier even exists. Pastor and staff feel pressure because of the amount of effort required to manage a church with a multitude of ministries that have been generated over time to keep up with the needs of a diverse and growing population of members, and created to facilitate outreach into the community and the world. Phones ring non-stop, counseling piles up, and meetings run into other meetings. But the greatest creator of tension at this level is the realization that things are falling through the cracks.

The management style of just adding more circles to increase ministry has become unmanageable (see chapter three). The pastor is no longer free to be a leader, but instead has become a manager of what has been built and may not be a very good one at that. The pastor feels like the guy on the Ed Sullivan Show (showing my age) who spins the plates. As the plates' spinner adds disc after disc, excitement builds as the audience waits for a plate to drop. It makes for a great show but a tough life. Eventually, a plate or two does hit the ground. On the Sullivan Show, the plates were pottery; in the church the plates are people.

If the elders notice anything, it is that elders' meetings seem to run longer and longer, and completing an entire agenda is rare. There is a reason for this. In the medium church, elders are making ministry decisions. These decisions are carried out in the daily life of the church. By the time a church reaches 700 or 800, there are a number of pastors on staff, all leading sections of the church, and all needing decisions to be made in order to carry on the ministry. Since those decisions are made primarily by the elders, the hands of the pastors are effectively tied as they wait for decisions to be made. Agendas, therefore, get longer and longer. Elders who have been in that position since the 100/200 days may feel they have returned to the old days.

Sometimes elders chafe under the weight of the growing number of decisions to be made, especially since they feel more and more distant from the actual function of ministry. They may feel they need more information to make good decisions, information not always readily given since meeting time is limited and decisions demand to be made. Clearly, the role of the elders in making decisions regarding the daily operation of the church and the alignment of the staff in relation to ministry, needs to be revisited in order for this tension to be eased. Mounting tension of this type signals the approach of a barrier to growth.

B. The People

Much like the 100/200 barrier, members of a church approaching 700/800 feel like they are getting less ministry and attention than they did formerly. While each pastor on staff has areas of responsibility, the "taking care of people" part is largely determined by the people, whose propensity is to receive from their pastor of choice. Someone working in the children's ministry may like the way the youth pastor counsels and go to that pastor for help. Another serving on the worship team runs into financial trouble and seeks help from the outreach pastor since that pastor handles money well.

Managing ministries, being available to leaders, and connecting with people according to their whim is fine when the church is at 500 or so, but at 700/800 a new management style is needed that is somewhat more directive for the people. Remember, releasing more people into ministry will keep the church in its pattern of growth. But when pastors become managers *of* ministry instead of equippers *for* ministry, growth potential is inhibited and people fall through the cracks.

2. The Paradigm—The Roles of Pastors and Elders Will Have to Change.

A. The Elders

The most difficult shift for elders to make is this one, but it is vital that it be made if the church is going to break this barrier. Two simultaneous processes must occur. First, the elders must move from being decision-makers to becoming policy-makers. Second, the circles of ministry (diagramed in

Chapter Three) must be regrouped into circles of circles, and the pastoral configuration must be realigned to facilitate this. We'll look at each in turn.

Policies govern decisions. Policies are decisions themselves, but at "macro" level—a philosophical level. Policies are like railroad tracks. Someone at the executive level in the railroad company decided where they would provide service and what type of business they were looking for. They would haul logs or cattle. They would service auto makers or shipyards. In the end, these philosophical discussions led to the laying of track. After the tracks were laid, engineers would decide how many cars to connect to a given engine.

Further, the conductor would make decisions concerning the schedule. Another person would decide the menu and shop accordingly. It is clear that the policies made at the executive level dictated the type of service provided and where. After that, thousands of smaller decisions are made daily by the people actually running the train to cause quality rail service to occur. It would be absurd to think the railroad executives would meet daily to decide the menu for the following day. Elders beyond 800 must become policy makers. They lay track for the pastors to follow and release them to make the daily decisions in order to provide "quality rail service."

In the church under 800, elders make ministry decisions and are over ministry. In the church beyond 800, elders make policy decisions; the staff is over ministry, making decisions collectively at times, much like an eldership in a medium-sized church.

In order to circumvent the growing confusion caused by the multiplication of ministry circles, a church only has two choices: 1. stop adding new ministry and bring growth to a halt, or 2. reconfigure pastoral alignment. As I mentioned in Chapter Three, this reconfiguration requires restructuring circles of ministry into circles of circles.

There is no set way to design these circles of circles, since the style and function of each church will dictate how these structures are built. A departmental church will structure differently than a cell-based church. A departmental church that is a teaching center will configure differently than a departmental church whose philosophy of ministry is outreach oriented.

The point here is to see the big picture and build the paradigm to fit your church's style and function. Think groupings, but always keep in mind that releasing people into ministry is our main job. In the long run this is what provides growth, because this is what matures people. Structures either inhibit or promote this process. When the structures that used to release people now inhibit that flow, they must be changed. Look for the places where people fall through the cracks. Look for places where two pastors cover the same ground.

Look for natural lines of demarcation. Some churches build their groupings departmentally—all education in circle "A," for example. Under that might be children's ministry, adult Sunday School, home groups (in a teaching-oriented church), etc. Perhaps outreach would fall under category "B" including such things as visitation, greeters, evangelism, home groups (in an evangelistically-oriented church), etc. Pastoral care might be under category "C" covering the areas of singles, youth, counseling, etc. I mentioned earlier that our church is a cell church.

Some cell churches break their communities up into geographic districts and place their people and cells under pastors by zip code or zone. Others break their cells into categories, much like a departmental church, and group types of cells by category under various pastors. The easiest way to build circles of circles is to follow the natural lines of demarcation.

B. The People

It will take some adjustment on the part of the people to get used to doing things a new way. Church life beyond 800 is simply different than church life at 500. Fellowship, discipleship, evangelism, worship, etc. are all the same, but the way in which these occur is different at this level.

The clearest example of how things have changed is in the area of communication. In most medium churches, while pastors have specific job descriptions, the people get used to going to their favorite source for counsel and information. They simply expect all the pastors to be up on everything going on in the church. "Ya'll work there (our church is in the South) all together, I just figured you'd know what was goin' on."

In a church over 800, structures and the lines of communication that support them must become clearer. While this is a hassle to those used to church life another way, it is for their benefit that these changes be made. Sending people to the right people allows for a higher quality product. A larger church requires a higher degree of specialization from its pastors. This means if you talk to a pastor serving in District One, that pastor may have no clue about what is happening in District Two, but can answer anything you ask about District One. People get better service, and they are better known and cared for as specialization increases. Fewer people fall through the cracks.

3. The Personnel—We Must Create Another Tier of Pastoral Leadership in the Church.

A. The Elders

"What's wrong with the way we have it configured now? It seems to be working." Of course that is what the elders will feel since the 700/800 barrier is tougher on the pastoral staff than it is on them, as opposed to the 100/200 mark which specifically pinches elders. The elders need to see that there must be a realignment that will, by necessity, change the way the pastors relate to the eldership and to each other. In the medium church, all the pastors, with the exception of the Senior Pastor, are likely to be on the same plane. While they all perform different jobs, they all only relate as subordinates to one person, the Senior Pastor.

When a church realigns the circles of ministry into circles of circles, some pastors will wind up over others on the organizational chart. This is necessary for two reasons: 1. The Senior Pastor can return to functioning as a leader instead of a manager, since the management responsibilities belong to the new tier of leaders on the "District" or larger "Department" level, and 2. Creating a new level of leadership will focus the responsibilities of those leaders into clearly defined areas, increasing accountability, closing cracks, and providing more opportunity for people to be released into ministry.

To effectively run a district or mega-department, a leader will have to raise up new leaders into ministry. Suppose a baseball team divided into three. The single team formerly had one short stop, one first baseman, one catcher, etc. Now that the team is three, each position must be filled on each team. Now three short stops are needed, three first basemen, three catchers, etc.

How do we decide who the new District Pastors or Departmental Pastors will be? Remember, in realigning the staff in this way, you have created another level of leadership; therefore, these positions must be filled by people who are leaders. I like to think of the folks who fill these slots as people who could be Senior Pastors themselves. They may not be gatherers in the sense that they have the gift to take a church to this level, but they need to be people who are capable of leading/managing a large and growing number of people. As the church continues to grow, the pastors on this tier will be responsible for hundreds (possibly thousands) of people, and a number of pastors working under them. The wrong leader, one who does not have the capacity to operate at this level, could hinder growth.

It is possible that in realigning, new positions may have to be created, and new pastors brought on staff to fill these slots. In our case, we were not in a position to hire these folks right away. We drew in the positions on the organizational chart and temporarily penciled existing pastors into more than one slot. These pastors were required for a time to wear more than one hat. Recognizing that these infrastructural changes would produce growth, and therefore an increase in finances, we established a priority list for hiring new pastors and support personnel. As funds were available, we brought on the required individuals.

B. The People

How you communicate these changes to the people is crucial. Shared the wrong way, the members are likely to feel they are losing their pastor and being shuffled off to some low grade associate. People must be led and fed. If these two are in place, they will follow a leader anywhere. I had these two principles in mind when I first told the congregation of the shifts we were making.

Before I addressed the congregation on the specifics of the radical adjustments we were making, I firmly established in their minds that we were growing, and that growth was a good thing. Then I assured them that in the future, they would continue to be fed. "As you know we are growing. And since we are committed to providing quality pastoral care for you and your family, we are going to make some changes. As we grow, we don't want pastoral care to get further away from you. As it stands right now, it is harder and harder to get to me. I have to make appointments with myself! We want pastoral care to be closer and more accessible to you." You can see that these words speak to the issue of feeding; sheep want to be cared for. They need shepherding.

Not only must sheep be fed; they must be led. I presented to them the manner in which we had devised a provision for more effective pastoral care. "As of November 1st, we are dividing the county into three districts and establishing a District Pastor over each. Each person, therefore, as of that day, will have a personal pastor. Whereas it has been increasingly difficult to get to me, it is the job of these pastors to be available to you. They will marry your children and bury your parents. They will visit you in the hospital and counsel you as needed.

"I, on the other hand, will no longer do pastoral counseling. My role will be to lead the church into all God has called us to and do my very best to empower these pastors to be the best they can be in serving you and releasing you into the ministry to which you have been called." I further outlined the new configuration, detailing how these changes would provide greater opportunity for all to come into maturity by being released into greater levels of ministry. The new changes were enthusiastically embraced and growth was the result. The barrier was broken.

It is easier to start a thing than it is to maintain it! Members and staff must be trained to function in the new paradigm. For instance, when people called the office looking for a pastor with whom they could talk, our staff was trained to ask, "Do you know who your District Pastor is?" If the caller did not, each staff member was equipped with a card outlining the zip codes of each district. Budgets were drafted and monies spent along district lines. The districts for us are almost like three churches within one church, so each person on staff had to be trained to think in terms of districts, not just Manna Church. Over time, both staff and congregation got it. But even now, we are training new members, and sometimes reminding old ones how to relate in a life-giving way to our structure.

The chart on page 46 breaks churches into three size categories. In each category, the infrastructure of the church functions differently from the others. What happens when an elder or pastor is functioning in the wrong "size category?" What if multiple leaders are functioning in different "size categories?" Tension in churches develops along two lines. First, tension points are produced by growth barriers, which has been the subject of this chapter. Second, the most damaging and most severe tension is caused by the improper alignment of pastors and elders in reference to their relative size. This is the topic of the next chapter.

CHAPTER FIVE

Tension Produced by Improper Alignment

Unfortunately, I have seen it too many times. And routinely, when I talk about it in pastors groups, attendees roll their eyes as I outline the scenario. The all too familiar scene takes place wherever elders' meetings are held in a church that has begun to approach the 100/200 barrier. As described in the last chapter, tension mounts as the church draws near the first, major growth roadblock. As the elders' discussion turns to what it will take for the church to go to the next level, invariably, the pastor and an elder or two are already there. They recognize the need to change internal operations and hire staff. But the rub is exactly "how" and "who?"

As the meeting grinds on, and opinions are expressed, there is often one voice that undercuts the whole process and takes the church back into the "dark ages," leaving her stuck under the shadow of the seemingly impenetrable "200 wall." Whenever this voice expresses itself, it will usually win the day. I can hear it now. One leader sits quietly, listening to the discussion on the present state of affairs in the church, and finally speaks. "Brothers, do you remember the days when things were so much easier? Remember when we gathered as friends in Pastor Jim's living room? We would talk and pray and just let the Holy Spirit lead us. We did the work together and loved it. Now look at us, we meet in the conference room and talk church business the whole time. We are so busy and so pressured. Brothers, we need to get back to the old days. Remember when brother so and so did such and such?" Every one laughs, bitten by the nostalgic bug, fogging the brain and intoxicating the heart with memories of days when life seemed better.

At this point, the pastor and one forward-looking elder feel the moment, the meeting, and the momentum slipping away. While everyone else considers "how we got here—in this mess," the pastor tries to convince all that "how we got here" is the right question, but to view it as an opportunity! However, the pastor will likely lose the day. The pastor will go home, frustrated, and on the way call the one forward-looking elder on the cell phone.

These are kinds of situations that cause pastors to want to give up, and in fact, many do. The numbers on pastoral burnout, depression, and departure from ministry in America today are staggering. Elders also suffer. These folks work secular jobs and serve in the church as a means of serving the Lord. Most have never been to Bible College or served in full-time ministry. Most are too busy to keep up with all the current literature on how to lead or grow a church. They even find it difficult to keep up with all the stuff going on in their own local churches. They are simply the best people in the church—they serve, tithe, volunteer, support, and sacrifice without asking for praise or recognition.

In the situation described above, neither the pastor nor the elders realize what is happening. All of them have great hearts and are doing their best to move the church forward and honor the Lord. All of them already feel the pressure produced by a barrier they probably don't even know exists. And now, an even more damaging pressure has entered into their midst, robbing their unity and potentially destroying their relationships. The trouble is simple. The Pastor and one elder have moved over into thinking like a medium-sized church even though they may not be able to articulate that fact. They see what needs to be done and intuitively respond to the present condition of the church by suggesting change.

The others are still in the small church mindset and simply cannot see how change will help. Then the one well-meaning elder wins the emotion of the moment with the head-in-the-sand argument, effectively shutting down any growth thinking in the group. The real difficulty here, however, is not that they leave the meeting without a plan. The real difficulty is that they leave divided, not over the issue, but in their thinking and in relation to one another, to ministry, and to how decisions should be made. The Pastor and one elder are in "medium" and rest of the eldership is in "small." The greatest tension is yet to come.

In fact, the most severe and potentially damaging tensions are those caused by pastors and individuals on the leadership team who relate to the church out of the wrong size category. Problems caused by this type of situation are among the main reasons I am called in to help a church. I see these types of improper alignment in all manner of situations. There is the one elder in a large church who still thinks with a small church mindset and carries the expectations associated with the small church. This elder wants to handle stuff that should no longer be controlled at that level. I have seen local churches led by a pastor with a large-church mindset in a small-church context. Having a vision to be a large church is great, but you can't skip the stages necessary to get there. In the pastor's impatience, structures have been implemented prematurely which tax the leadership team and cause the people to feel, in effect, "unpastored." In many situations, the pastor and individuals on the leadership team are literally all over the chart on page 46. It is no wonder that tensions result when they try to make decisions or do ministry together!

I have heard some of the most hurtful things said by the best of people, each accusing the other's motive and yet each with a heart burning for the church to experience God's best. Confused as to the roles of both pastor and elders in the church, uncertain of how decisions are to be made and where the lines of authority are to be drawn, gridlock develops and, like a partisan Congress, great people take sides. Relationships suffer, unity is broken, church politics develops, and momentum for growth is lost. How can we avoid such a calamity?

1. Education
Produces Liberation

Simply put, the truth sets free. Both pastor and elders need to recognize where they really are in the growth and life of the church. Often when I go over the "chart" with pastors and their eldership team, the result is confession and reconciliation. Honest discussion develops when people recognize what is happening.

Often, local churches do not have accurate records of where they are numerically. In such cases, the Senior Pastor guesses and sees 300, while the negative elder who calls himself a realist, sees 150. If the truth be told, both are probably wrong. How can they hope to lead the church properly if they have no

> *The most severe and potentially damaging tensions are those caused by pastors and individuals on the leadership team who relate to the church out of the wrong size category.*

honest appraisal of where they are? Decide on what an active member is and count each week. Keep good records and measure trends.

I have heard all kinds of objections to counting over the years. "God will judge the church if you count." The context for this idea is drawn from David's ill-fated effort to determine the military strength of Israel. His count amounted to a passive rejection of God as their Commander-in-Chief, the One who formerly fought for them. If your motive for counting it to establish your own importance in comparison to the other nations (local churches in your city), then repent. If counting is a sin, then God is guilty. He counted the men of war in Israel, the number who died in various plagues, the 12 disciples, the 70, and the 120 in the Upper Room. He claimed 500 saw His Son alive after His death. He counted the people who responded to Peter's in-your-face altar calls in the early chapters of Acts. He even counts the number of hairs on our heads! I think He is okay if we choose to count the number of people who attend our services, in an effort to find a reliable yardstick to measure the effectiveness of our service to Him.

Once a clear understanding of "how many we are" is developed, we need to come into agreement as to where the church is located on the chart—small, medium, large. Be careful to analyze not just the numbers, but the mechanisms by which ministry is done and decisions are made.

2. Communication Produces Cooperation

In all likelihood, there will be various pastors or elders on the team who are not operating or thinking out of the right context—the small-church mindset elder in a medium church, the large-church-minded pastor in a 150 member setting, etc. The trouble is that most will not see themselves accurately. Rather than directly confront each other, it is important that all recognize the fact that we are often the last to see ourselves correctly. In addition, we must see ourselves through the eyes of others in order to gain an accurate picture. A finger-point and I-told-you-so session is only going to hurt feelings and damage relationships.

In order to mature, we are instructed by Scripture to speak the truth in love to one another (see Eph. 4:15). Love in this setting demands we take the non-confrontational approach. A generic discussion of how things ought to be done, how ministry is to be conducted, and how decisions are made at the stage in church development will create an atmosphere where the group can decide what the future will look like. In embracing the future and agreeing on how the pastor/elder team will relate, the members of the group are, in effect, turning from the past. I am not advocating ignoring the scriptural admonitions to clear offenses. I firmly believe that unforgiveness, bitterness, and resentment must be dealt with in a biblical manner, but never in a group context.

Each church is unique and has its own personality. Exactly how the individuals work together must be determined by the group itself. In the same way, who is over what, and who answers to whom is very organic. There is no way this, or any book, can specifically outline the particulars of these dynamics in a given setting. But once a leadership team has accurately defined where the church is and openly communicated concerning how they will relate both now and in the future, a spirit of cooperation is established. They may not be meeting any longer in Pastor Jim's living room, but the same life is now fueling the meetings once again. Unity is the order of the day, and momentum is recovered. Best of all, their relationships are mended and strong once again. If the infrastructure, the bones of the church is healthy, the rest of the body can grow. Communication produces cooperation.

3. Expectation is Invitation

The most powerful by-product of being on the same page is found in the idea that expectation produces invitation. Once we know where we are, we are able to see where we are going. With those two items in place, the visionaries go to work, devising a plan to take the church to the next level. Remembering the ideas concerning bringing a vision to pass (as discussed in chapter one), the elders and pastors are able to create a plan to facilitate that vision, with specific reference to where the church is today. The exciting thing about this is that all involved recognize they are not dealing with a pipedream but a real vision with teeth. This plan is based in facts—facts all parties have agreed upon.

Visions are brought to pass on the strength of unity, as Nehemiah's "Threefold Law of Vision" dictates (Chapter One). People work for what they own and the best way to lead people to own a plan is to enlist them in developing it. Even though the plan may be long term, a church at 350 outlines the steps to move toward 700. For example, elders and pastors alike are confident since they can see the end and the steps to get there. If the plan needs adjustment along the way, the team has the tools in hand to measure growth and address needs as they arise.

One of the important items a leadership team can expect is the approach of a new barrier, and the tension they know will develop. If they are able to recognize that dynamic ahead of time, they will be able to implement change in stages as they draw nearer to the anticipated barrier. Discussions may be held well in advance of the roadblock, and strategies developed to move them right through. In discussing the 200 barrier, I heard Peter Wagner quote one of his students, Rick Warren, the now famous pastor of the giant Saddleback Community Church, as saying, "The best way to break the 200 barrier is to never stop for it." Assess where you are. Communicate with the team. Get everyone on the "same page" and develop a plan. Use this plan as a tool, as a device to guide toward growth, anticipating tension, and navigating through barriers.

Every time I meet with a group of pastors or with the leaders in a local church, a host of questions always follow the seminar, the most common of which will be answered in the next chapter.

CHAPTER SIX

"So, What About...?"
(Answers to Frequently Asked Questions)

At the end of every seminar with pastors or "strategy talk" with pastors and local church leaders, there always follows an ad hoc question and answer session. No two of these sessions are the same, since each is tailored to the individual dynamics involved in a particular church or group of churches. Three topics, phrased in terms of specific questions, are common.

1. "Who should I bring on staff to help break the next barrier?"

This question is almost always asked by leaders of churches under 200, and is often framed in another way, "I have this really great youth guy (or music guy, or retired guy or "something" guy) who works for us part-time. Maybe I should just make him full-time, and he will help us break this barrier." Pastor may have an unspoken promise of future employment that they are trying to avoid breaking. Perhaps they see an inexpensive way to accomplish their barrier-breaking goal. Or maybe they are just looking for the fastest way over the wall. But it is here that pastors should slow down and back up, because this is by far the most important hire they'll ever make. This decision will determine whether the church will break this barrier or not.

Just because a guy is a really great guy does not mean that is the person who should become "Number Two" in the transition from the "Shepherd Model" to the "Rancher Model." As has already been said, this person needs to be the kind of person that the church members can look to in an authoritative/pastoral role—as a shepherd. Maybe the worship leader is that person. Maybe the youth leader is that person. But one thing is for sure. He isn't that person simply because he appears to be next in line by virtue of longevity or the fact that he presently occupies a part-time staff position.

This is the place where a good number of churches make the mistake that will forever keep them on the small side of this barrier. At 180 or so, most churches only have the funds to pay two full-time pastors. Often, as soon as they reach this mark, numerically or financially, they run right out and buy themselves one of the two traditional first hires—a music person or a youth person. If they are fortunate, they may have hired an individual who can also fill the shoes of a shepherd to the church. Most often, however, they get what they bought— a really great music leader or a young person who is loved by youth and parents alike, and not a second shepherd-type pastor.

My advice? It is always better to have a "jack of all trades and a master of none" as your "second" and use volunteers with your youth and worship until you break the 200 barrier, unless the youth or worship person has the ability to serve both in their specialized ministry and wear the shepherd's hat as well. "So how can I tell if my youth guy has that capacity?" You cannot measure that according to that individual's desire or your vision for their life. You can always tell a leader by whether or not they have a following. Do people outside the scope of that person's ministry follow? Are people in the church, though not directly under that person, attracted to them? Do they seek that person out? If the answer is yes, you have a leader on your hands. Hire away! If not, leave that person in their present position and allow them time to develop without the pressure of being expected to provide what they cannot yet give.

2. "What do I do with an elder who cannot 'make the jump' to the next level?"

In other words, what is a pastor to do if there is an elder or staff member whose mindset is stuck in small, while the church is functioning in medium, or in medium while the church is functioning in large? This question has to be answered on several levels.

First, this is always going to be the case in a growing church. As a church develops and moves from one level to the next, people adapt to change and to changing structures at

different rates. The rate of personal adaptation is not determined by a person's intelligence or commitment to the vision, but rather by their temperament and personality, both
of which have been given to them by God. As leaders, we
are required by God to provide an environment where people

> *As a church develops and
> moves from one level to the
> next, people adapt to change
> and to changing structures
> at different rates.*

can embrace change and work through the ramifications associated with that change in their own souls.

Second, it should be noted that without pressure, everything naturally reverts to form. Leaders sometimes labor
through the process of determining that change is necessary,
building a consensus among the elders toward that end, only
to abandon the process once a conclusion has been made,
falsely assuming that everyone is forever on board. When in
the following week's board meeting one or more elders "re-
vert to form" and function in the old way of thinking, the
visionary leaders, who long ago moved to the next level in
their minds, cannot believe their ears. Mutiny! "Where were
these people last week? Didn't they hear anything we said?"

Of course they did, but in both the short and long runs, the process will have to be revisited and leaders reminded that they all agreed to operate in a different paradigm, and why this is good for all. Leading is our job. It is a process.

Third, there are those who seem incapable or unwilling to change the way they function. These people have built a wall around what "is" as if it will always be, and refuse to recognize that their "is" has become a "was." Amazingly, they are oblivious to the fact that the rest of us have moved on. For church members to be this way is okay, but leaders who refuse to grow and change with the group become roadblocks, and they must be removed.

Caution! How you remove the roadblock is a statement of the type of leader you are. Many unprincipled leaders simply remove these people from the positions they hold and discard them like some disposable product whose expiration date has past. For them, the forward progress of the organization is the highest value they hold. Please remember, these people who refuse to grow, however troublesome to us as pastors, are still people, loved and purchased by God at the cost of His Son. There is a treasure in that earthen vessel. They cannot be simply removed. They must be repositioned.

There may come a time when elders can no longer serve in that capacity, simply because they have chosen to live in the past. While they have made themselves no longer useful to the eldership team, they are still useful to God. It is our job as leaders to help these people find the slot in the church that will allow them to prosper and continue to serve as a *"joint that supplies according to the working of each individual part"* (see Eph. 4:16). I would suggest a series of open and honest conversations between the Senior Pastor and the elder in question, the point of which is to find the place where the elder can serve and grow—a place where that person can experience fulfillment and excitement in making a contribution to the body.

3. What if the church is not growing at all?

The pastors and leaders who ask this question know that the problem in the church is not a growth problem—that they have bumped up against a barrier—but a non-growth problem. Something has gone wrong, and the church has plateaued at a certain level, or worse, is in decline. The answer to this question could be volumes in length and include many works written by others who are experts in the field of church growth. In approaching the question and in anticipation of researching to find the answer, it is wise for leaders to break the church, on paper, into three parts: 1. front door, 2. function and operations, and 3. back door. I will deal with each in turn.

The Front Door
Before we begin dismantling everything in the church and copying the megachurch whose testimony we just read, we should examine how we are doing with our "front door." The first question I always ask is, "What is your lead count?" In other words, "How many visitors do you have each week?" (Forgive the secular terminology. I believe there are both a science and a Spirit aspect to growing a church. Combine the two, and the church will grow. Neglect one, and the church will suffer.) Without new people coming, how can any church

grow? If there are only a few visitors per week, then I would suggest focusing the research in areas pertaining to attracting newcomers. Advertising a great preaching series, holding a "Friend Day," sponsoring a neighborhood or city-wide festival, engaging in servant evangelism or other outreach projects, and creating invitation cards for members to distribute are all ways, among many others, to increase traffic in our Sunday services.

Once we examine the flow of newcomers and discuss ways to increase that flow, the next "front door" question that must be asked is this, "What is your assimilation process like?" This is a big topic! (We once held a half-day seminar on this topic alone, for our network of churches!) If people are coming, what are you doing to encourage them to stay? How do they connect with the church? Do you have a process, a system, in place to follow up on those who visit? Are they greeted in the parking lot, at the door? How do you address newcomers in the service? Do you embarrass them? How do you find out who is there? Is there a guest card? How do you get the card to them? How do you retrieve the card? What do you do with this information after you retrieve it? Do you have a formal membership? How do people become members? Is this information readily available to newcomers? How many hoops do new people have to jump through to become a part of your church? Are the staff and volunteers trained to help facilitate the assimilation process and answer any questions guests may have?

I encourage churches to determine their philosophy of membership—what is required for new people to connect with the church—and develop a *system* to facilitate this. Simply putting some really great people on the task requires constant maintenance and oversight, since the procedure is only people-driven. One pastor told me, "Oh, we have a great assimilation process. We have a lady who takes all the cards and contacts the visitors herself every Sunday afternoon." I asked, "What if she is sick or on vacation?" He has a procedure that is very dependent on one person to make it happen. He had no system.

A system runs all by itself. Wal-Mart has a system for receiving returned merchandise. It is the same in every store. Wal-Mart is known for quality service, not because they hire really sweet people, but because they have a system. People are trained to operate the system into which the value of customer service has been built. When you fly from city to city, the airline knows which seat you occupy not because a really smart counter agent remembered you, but because they have a system. Create a system to facilitate the assimilation of new members into the church. Frustrated at one point, I took a pastor friend to lunch who was known for keeping a large number of those who came to his church. I furiously took notes as he outlined his whole process to me. Then, I returned to the office and modified much of what he said to fit our church context. I created a system. Now, we simply train folks to work the system (with plenty of customer service built in!)

Functions and Operations

I'm sorry but some churches are just weird. They don't grow, because they scare people away. Joseph Aldrich said that the main barrier to evangelism is not theological but cultural. I agree. Every church has its own tradition, even if their tradition is "non-tradition." There is nothing wrong with tradition, even if that tradition is based on a departure from the lifeless religion of our past. The unfortunate thing is that often we ascribe theological meaning to what began as a pragmatic structure employed to facilitate life. The result is a "sacred cow," a religious structure without which we cannot conceive of "doing church."

When the church was meeting in the pastor's living room it was appropriate to go around the circle and ask members to introduce the friends they brought to the meeting, but now that we meet in public with 300 people present, this procedure is embarrassing to the unsuspecting people who come, and the poor folks who brought them. When everyone knew everyone, and Old Bob would sometimes take off down the middle aisle during worship just because he had a "quickening," all would knowingly smile at the harmless old brother who had his spiritual upbringing in a small Pentecostal farm revival. But now folks are afraid to bring family and friends, because they don't want to be cast in that light. I am not against the move of the Spirit, but as one friend puts it, "If it is God for one; it is God for all." When only the same, select few are the ones who feel the move, I wonder if it is really a move or simply a religious exercise. David Morris, author and well-known worship leader used to say, "Worship is free for all, but worship is not a free-for-all."

Learn to ask "why" about the stuff you do in your services and in the daily operation of the church. What do you do best? Make sure you put your best foot forward. Center on your strengths; put them up front. Is worship weak? Feature teaching. Is your children's ministry strong? Play that card more often. Mobilize in the areas you are strong and build in the areas you are weak. If, in asking "why," you uncover a "sacred cow" or two, kill it and invite the neighborhood to a huge feast. It will increase your lead count and help the church grow.

Back Door

Some churches lose folks as fast as they gain them. As new members are being added, old members are walking out the back door. Shutting the back door is not that hard. The key to keeping members in the church is not great worship or great preaching. These, and other aspects of ministry, might be what attracted people to your church, but they are not the reasons they stay. Thank God! It is overwhelming to think that every Sunday we must re-compete to keep members in the church by hitting a "home run" sermon or producing a new set of goose bumps with every song. People stay in a church because they have relationships with the people in the church!

If your back door is open, your structures designed to facilitate the development and maintenance of relationships are failing. Some churches have no intentional structure designed to promote relationships. When a church is very small, no intentional structure is needed, but as it grows, leaders must pay attention to this vital aspect of church life. The church is not primarily an institution or a religious organization, and it is definitely not a building. The church is people. While folks might be attracted to a church because of what it offers, they stay because of the friendships they develop there.

As I mentioned earlier, our church is a cell church. Every Sunday we meet for public worship, but other than that, everything we do is done in the cell context. (In fact, even on Sunday mornings, our children's ministry is built on a cell framework.) One of the prime reasons we chose this format as a blueprint for building our church was the fact that the cell concept is highly relational. The life of the cell is the flow of ministry in that cell, and true ministry flows along relational lines. Without strong relationships, cell groups will fail. So, if the cells are working, then relationships must be strong.

A church does not have to be a cell church to build strong relationships, but it must be intentional in seeing that an environment has been created that is conducive to fellowship and friendship-building. Meetings, events, and ministry tasks must have relational time built into them. Those minutes at the beginning of a board meeting when it seems impossible to get the folks to stop fellowshipping with each other are far from wasted. In fact, depending on the agenda, they may be the most important minutes in the meeting! Picnics, parties, cookouts, retreats are great times for people to connect with each other.

Even ministry events can be relational in nature. Our church is very aggressive in evangelism. In additional to regular on-going evangelism, every year we hold a number of large events. We put people into teams, allowing for plenty of interaction among team members. Side by side they labor in the same vineyard, passing out cold soft drinks at a city event, washing cars, or perhaps distributing tracts. They battle the same difficulties and experience the victories—together. *Together* is the key. Then all the teams gather back at the church building and share reports. The whole thing has a "family" feel. We are building memories together. It would be so much easier to see the task of evangelism as a monolithic function—reach the lost. But if it, or any other ministry function, is framed carefully, it accomplishes two goals: 1. perform ministry, and 2. build relationships.

Examine the structure of the ministries in the church, asking key questions. Is this ministry built in such a way as to promote the building of friendships among those who participate? Are people only involved in this ministry because they are committed to it, or do some come because they enjoy the fellowship as well as the ministry? Do these people get together for fellowship outside the confines of ministry? Remember, people stay in a church because they are committed to each other, not to the mission or vision of the church. Do not kid yourself, plenty of other churches in town have great vision and wonderful ministries, but they don't have the relationships that your members have developed over the years. Those relationships are with the friends who attend your church!

A great test to see how you are doing in this area is found before and after every service and every meeting in your church. Do the people come late and leave as soon as it is over, or do they hang around and hang out? Are they hard to gather for the meeting, or do they sit silently waiting for it to start? Is the roar of fellowship so loud that someone has to whistle or yell to get their attention? I often commend the people for being hard to gather. I want them to love fellowship; they need it, and others are attracted to it. Ted Haggard spoke at one of our conferences and intuitively diagnosed the health of our network based solely on the fact that the crowd came early to hang out and would never leave when the meetings finished! The stronger the relationships in a local church, the greater the retention rate. Understanding this dynamic is no doubt one of the reasons Ted leads such a large church with such a small back door!

CHURCH LIFE IS
A TEAM SPORT

Senior Pastors multiply themselves through proper alignment with leadership teams. The leadership team rises to a level of usefulness in the body which they would never have attained otherwise, when they function in right relationship to the Senior Pastor. When this happens, the body is better able to operate in its calling and produce growth on its own. The leadership of a church, like the bone structure of a natural body, needs to be healthy and properly aligned in order for the body to work as it should. Teamwork in the leadership promotes teamwork in the body and that is what church life is all about—the body, "building itself up in love" (see Eph. 4:16). As local leaders release the Senior Pastor to lead, and as the Senior Pastor allows the leaders to help, the church will be positioned to pass through each barrier they face and enjoy the ministry as they do it!

There are two reasons for growing a local church. The first is to produce a vehicle through which the kingdom of

God may advance on the earth. The growth of a local church can become a goal in itself. When that happens, its leadership has fallen into idolatry. Jesus established the church to further His cause in Jerusalem (the local area), Judea/Samaria (the region), and the uttermost parts of the earth. We seek growth for our churches so we can fulfill this mission more effectively—period. No other motive is acceptable. We aren't after bigger churches so the pastor can build a name, or so members may increase their impression of prestige in the community.

In addition, when the leadership of a church makes growth its number one aim, they miss the real secret of that growth and actually undercut the process. If they focus, however, on growing people and releasing them into ministry (the second reason for growing a church), the natural result is numerical increase in the church. For room to be made for people to come into their destiny through service, the internal structures of the church will have to change. When these structures are readjusted and the leaders are properly aligned, more room is created for others. Growth results. Growth brings with it a need for change. Again, internal structures are readjusted and leaders realigned, creating more room for others. Again, growth results. It is a wonderful cycle leading to expansion on increasing scales.

God intended it to be this way. He never envisioned a small company of superstars extending His Kingdom in the earth. From the start, He saw a body—His Body—with many members, each doing its part to change the world.

" ...But, speaking the truth in love, may grow up in all things into Him who is the head—Christ—from whom the whole body, joined and knit   together by what every   joint supplies, according to the effective working by which every part does its share, causes growth of the body for the edifying of itself in love" (Eph. 4:15,16 NKJ).

In bolstering our numbers, not as spectators, but as players, we bolster our resources in our quest to extend the kingdom of God on the earth.

Christianity is a team sport. As we increase the number of players on the team, we increase the size of the team. In bolstering our numbers, not as spectators, but as players, we bolster our resources in our quest to extend the kingdom of God on the earth. Release people into their calling and restructure to contain continued growth, all for the glory of God!

SUBJECT INDEX